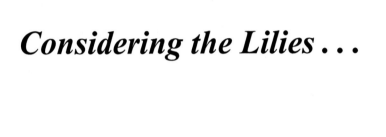

Considering the Lilies . . .

Library of Congress Control Number: 2013920355
ISBN: Hardcover   978-1-4931-2727-6
             Softcover   978-1-4931-2726-9
             eBook   978-1-4931-2728-3

All Illustrations in the book were done by Mrs. Patricia Brewer, http://www.patriciabrewerartist.com/

Author's photo, back cover, provided by Gus Grubba

This book was printed in the United States of America.

Rev. date: 12/11/2013

To order additional copies of this book, contact:
Xlibris LLC
1-888-795-4274
www.Xlibris.com
Orders@Xlibris.com
137239

Dedication

To my first cousin, Margaret Lucille (Lou) Covington

Commander United States Navy (Ret.)

Flight Nurse, Pacific Theater, World War II

Acknowledgments

Writing a book is never a one-person experience; therefore, I wish to express deep appreciation to the positive gentle people who have so helpfully joined in creating—start to finish—*Considering the Lilies*.

Special thanks go to Editor John Charles Robbins of the *Richmond County Daily Journal*, for granting permission for us to reprint a news story by Dawn M. Kurry, staff writer, published September 9, 2011. Subject of the report is Commander Margaret Lucille Covington, a Navy flight nurse of heroic service in World War IL The article is the last and the one true episode in the final stories herein.

Also, I'm grateful for the one-day answer to my request for a copy of the article from the Thomas H. Leath Memorial Library in Rockingham. Deborah Knight, librarian, supplied my need with gracious service and a much appreciated accompanying note.

Much gratitude goes to Suzanne Britt, who, with her brother and sister-in-law, shares the house we four call home. Suzanne is a writer and editor of renown, who reads copy, as good editors do. As she read this manuscript, some adverbs and adjectives had to go, as did a few exclamation points. Best of all, she suggested a section's transfer to a new chapter that was a perfect match. Bless her. A recently retired English professor, her final 25-year teaching prowess was claimed by Meredith College. Her own written words are still very much on the minds and hearts, as well as in the hands, of literary "faithfuls" in search of remarkable quotations originating in the depths of her knowledge and talent.

Pat and Fulton Brewer, husband-and-wife friends who never surrender to my work, always wanting to assist, deserve much appreciation. Artist among artists, Pat created the cover design, born of her originality for such work, and she also designed the artists' symbols of attention to the poetry herein. Artist? Writer as well. She's author of the "Foreword," an eloquently worded bridge (thank you, Pat), to her contribution of "The Last Word," which points to a futuristic hope for lilies to come, while giving the lilies of the field some human-like movements that draw all of us lilies closer to our Maker. Fulton has accepted the task of burning this manuscript onto a disc—at the request of the publisher. Where there's Fulton, there's technology.

Dinky and Dee Britt, Laura and Clyde Smith, Cindy O'Daniel, Ruth King, Caroline Warren, Pat and John Freeman, Pat and Bill Warren, and Mary and Earle Daeke have been the encouragers they always are.

Thank you so much. All of you.

Foreword

We all go through life collecting mental snapshots and anecdotes of family and friends, travels, and community. We all have stories, rich family histories, struggles, romances, and adventures. If we are at all aware of our surroundings, we absorb even more. Few of us, however, are able to write down the details creating settings, climate, and personalities of the characters as vividly as this author. In her final truth of her methods of observation, she realizes that observing the world changes our perception of it.

The beautifully written stories gathered here in *Considering the Lilies* are just a small part of a large collection of the writer's acquisition of events, happenings, and experiences extracted from life over her 85 years. Within these writings the author explores her own sensibility, remembrances, and detailed visions of life in the early 20th century in relation to her own metaphoric symmetry of the lily and her own life as a God created woman of the 21st century.

With family affection, discipline, humility and gratitude, her "lilies" described in this book met the hard demands of life in the early days of the twentieth century. This collection is based on the writer's keen allegiance to observation, an inherited familiarity with other people (in this case she calls them lilies) of bygone generations and a sensitive response to the sensuous beauty, and struggles, in their lives. This book reflects the author's ability to take even the most simple happening or event from her memory and turn it into an emotional, spiritual or blessed reflection, prayer of thanks for the lilies in your life and perhaps a smile to the reader.

Patricia Brewer

Contents

Considering the Lilies

By
Carolyn Covington Robinson

Considering the Lilies

The Beginning

Lily, my elderly mother, telephoned her also-elderly sister, "Sis," who was ill at her home in Tampa. Her daughter answered the phone. "How is she?" Mother asked the daughter. Nicki's response was delightful. Also, informative. "Oh, Lily, Mother 'toils not; neither doth she spin.'"

As a former church school teacher and lover of beautiful language, I've read again and again Jesus's one-sentence quotation regarding the "lilies of the field," which adds the grace of poetry to an already extraordinary address:

"Consider the lilies of the field, how they grow; they toil not, neither do they spin: and yet I say to you, that Solomon in all his glory was not arrayed like one of these."
(Mathew 6:28-29 KJV)

The biblical offering of "Consider the Lilies . . ." is central to the idea of this devotion, as are uses of poetry in blank verse and the final stories that subtly incorporate all these pages into the idea of paying tribute to women of the first half of the 20th Century.

A leap of faith dared me to compare the lilies of the field that neither "toiled" nor "spun" with the women who practiced those two exercises almost morning 'til night for most of their lives. Believing, I took the leap, assured as I was that the depth of my search would be the reward of my faith. How could it be? I was not profoundly committed to finding the Truth, but the Truth was my only goal. How can a "lily," whose membership is in the category of "humankind" relate to a lily of the plant family that, for example, is already dressed when it blooms? Furthermore, it grows by nourishment from the soil in which it lives and drinks the water of rain for its sustenance? The care God gives it sounds as if He blesses it mightily. He does bless *it* but not its *work*.

Human lilies throughout this piece are everywhere, and God blesses their work. Why? Because He has given us work to do in His world, making it natural for us to live—and, yes, worship with our minds and hands and hearts and voices. But, the plant lilies, that do not work? The truth I find is that the Creator blesses them—not for their work but for their workable contributions to His teachings. And their gifts are many, even though He uses them as examples of beauty and life as they respond to His gift of livelihood. Reread Jesus's commentary: "Consider the lilies of the field, how they grow; they toil not, neither do they spin: and yet I say to you, *that Solomon in all his [wealth and royal] glory was not arrayed like one of these.*" The quotation begins the value of Truth in truth.

My favorite study help is the *One Volume Bible Commentary,* edited by the Rev. J. R. Dummelow and first copyrighted in 1908. It teaches that "God provides for the birds without labour on their part, because labour is unnatural to birds. But labour is natural to [humankind]; therefore, God provides for [us] by blessing [our] labour." This thought also places specified flora (such as lilies) and fauna into the "labor as unnatural" category.

Contemplating the thought that God blesses the labor of humankind, I remember with great respect some of the women I've known for their work. Because of my young age during some difficult times, my observations reported here are not always firsthand; rather, I share what I've learned from both the observers and the observed. Clearly, the women from small southern towns like "those who saw me through" have remembered how, why, and for how long they "toiled" and "spun" with such grace. In paying tribute to them, I am convinced that they were instrumental in changing the culture of their (and our) limited world(s).

They tend their backyard gardens and their furrowed farm fields vast,

where men and women, children all, respect their farmland chores:

young daughters may milk Bessie, while their brothers learn to plow.

Some Lilies "put up" pickles (sweet), or beans. And all day long,

thank God for winter's storehouse.

"Lily" is the theme of this book. The logic is that through knowing women I never knew and talking over the hard times with those I never observed at work, I saw in them the same qualities of service, kindness, and determination as I admired in the "Lily Closest to Me."

The Closest Lily

Meet the closest Lily by turning your imagination back to a different time, another era. Think in terms of 1914, if you will, when Lily, at age 20, married her "Hubby," (Neal), who was 46, a month-to-the-day older than her own father.

The love affair began with a prelude to Neal's imagination which sounded forth majestically (but softly) as he stood outside his store rereading the striking new sign painted on the front window:

> ### *J. N. McNeill and Company*
> ### *Come in, please.*
> *We invite you to experience the ideal*
> *downtown-on-the-square market*
> *for choosing your staple and fancy groceries.*
> **[From 1910]**

But the following crescendo was louder—enough so that he lost interest in his own pride of having founded a successful business just a couple of years back—in 1910. Louder still, he heard it. Was he dreaming? Who was that beautiful young girl walking by? His timing lost its grip. "There goes my future wife," he said louder than he intended. "Who *was* she?" He'd find out. Determination set in. That very night he walked over to Jim's to pump information from his brother, the mayor. Jim knew the comings and goings of everybody in town. "Neal! Come on in. Libby's just putting a pie out to cool . . . ."

For once, Jim had no answers. But Lib, who surpassed her husband in awareness of the town's social life, filled him in. Of course, she, the official news gatherer for the local paper, would know. "The girl's name is Shannon," Lib started . . . .

Jim interrupted, "Hey! Now I get it. Her daddy's Libby's boss, you know: he's the new editor of the *Daily;* comes from Raleigh, no less. I hear his family wanted a slower pace—all those politicians, you know—state government, 'n all. I met him a couple of weeks ago. Name's Ben Linderman."

Neal cleared his throat as he squirmed in his chair, saying to his sister-in-law, "Lib, what can you tell me about her?"

"Nothing more, I guess. My gosh, Neal, she's a youngster."

A few days passed. And so did Shannon, coming or going by the store every day (her father had assigned her to a temporary summer job . . . . Of course! Any good dad would do that.)

Neal would create a way to meet her. He'd call on her parents. In fact, a night or two later, he walked just three blocks from home down a nice street to a pretty house with a town-owned tennis court on the adjoining property. A young couple played a match or two as Neal visited Shannon's parents on their front porch. (Was it Shannon playing tennis with that boy? His heart rate increased a little until he decided it wasn't she.)

That visit was the first of many with Shannon's mother and father, and all three seemed to enjoy each other. Occasionally, Shan—as she was more familiarly addressed—was at home, got to know Neal, and they, too, became at-ease acquaintances— even teasing each other as tennis adversaries.

Spring and summer passed before Neal called on Ben to confess his love for Shannon. He also admitted to wanting permission to marry her, adding confidently, "Don't worry about Shannon's future; she'll never want for *anything.* "

Ben and Mary were almost as impressed with that promise as with the difference in Neal and Shannon's ages. Only after months of seeing the older man and the very young woman grow in love and companionship, the parental blessing came.

They married on the Sunday before Easter under the long-leaf pines, for which Sandy Hills was noted. For the sacred event, all concerned preferred the local mid-town church in which each worshiped. On that day, Easter lilies were in profusion, coming close to stealing the show from the wedding party. As soon as the ceremony ended, Neal began his most ecstatic groom's language yet, calling his new wife "my Easter Lily." Before the reception ended, however, he cleverly reverted to a play on words as she became "MY SHANNA LILY," explaining that he had seen Canna Lilies growing, and *Shanna* was much more beautiful a name than *Canna*. Finally, he replaced his ardor with adoration, and "LILY" evolved into the name of the bride, and his "flower" bloomed forever as *Lily*.

Lily's name for Neal, however, was "Hubby," in the notion that she should never call her husband by his given name if her own father were a month younger than he. The whole incident was the practical reason for naming their very first child, a daughter, "Lil," who was born 14 years into their marriage. Ben exclaimed to Mary, "They really must love each other still to want a child born into their 'old age'."

Mary smiled through tears, adding, "Oh, that precious baby girl."

By the time Lil started to school, she and the grown-up McNeills left their lovely home, with all the amenities of a comfortable life, for a smaller house—but "nearer Lil's school." Money was slipping away.

Neal and two of his brothers were more ecstatic over the farmland's cotton crop that year than ever before. Each brother mortgaged his sizable land holdings to pay for the ginning of his prize yield. "It'll keep us solvent through whatever comes," vowed Neal's older brother, John. They rested briefly in that thought until it became fact that no miracle was going to reopen the gin. Neal was broken hearted, as were most of the Sandy Hills cotton growers. "My Lily, my Lily," he moaned to Jim and Lib. "And my young Lil," he added. "How will we make it?"

"The banks have failed!" so people cry tears of desperation.
Who among them ever dreamed of bread lines? Store shelves empty?
But also, there's the cotton crop unginned! The bills unpaid!
Whatever can we do to save our sanity? Our hope?
Oh, God, hold us to our faith.

When poor folks have to mortgage the last little that they have,
they all thank God for Lilies who will somehow make it through.
At Christmas one remarks with joy, "Of course we'll have a tree!"
Let's choose the luscious holly—Yes! the beauty by the porch—
"RED BERRY DECORATIONS!"

Lily, now an astute young woman of 44, made a decision without seeking Neal's advice. She went to her father, Ben, asking to borrow money to take the special business course being offered at Sandy Hills High School. Ben and Mary agreed immediately—their pleasure rooted in their daughter's competence, and in the excellent reports coming from the course and the school. Neal's emotional state at the Depression's financial holocaust was another reason to help their family any way they could, especially through their competent daughter. "We pray for you three, Lily. Bless you. All of you," offered Mary.

The grateful daughter whispered, "Thank you, my dears," as she embraced her parents. They wiped away tears, but Lily's confidence was sure. "I'll find a good job if there's one to be had," she declared. She aced the course and was employed almost immediately for a job which granted loans to struggling farmers. The salary was less than she had hoped, but what else was news those days?

A series of business closings followed, but Lily was seldom without a job and was grateful for each. She even worked in several short employments funded by the WPA, a new program of the Roosevelt Administration.

Neal became Lil's at-home dad. Lily was away at one job or another, with no public transportation but a county-owned bus line. Evenings, she was late getting back to Sandy Hills, but the driver let her out at her street, which intersected Main. Neal and Lil walked hand-in-hand to meet her bus, where the three greeted each other lovingly before again starting the two-block walk home.

Yes, Lily had a job, but when she came home in the evenings, much of her work began. Literally. While Neal prepared a simple dinner of, say, link sausages, grits, cornbread, and lima beans, mother and daughter planned their wardrobes for tomorrow, set up the ironing board, while Lily pressed the school clothes for Lil and the work clothes for herself. She also pressed the creases in Neal's trousers before or after the evening meal, whichever worked . . . . and pressed on . . . . 'til water heating was necessary for dishes, clothes, baths, shampoos, and Dad's daily beard removers.

When the family had opted for a smaller house, they found it to be small indeed; however, it was nestled in a bevy of Lil's first and second cousins who were uncannily close to her age. Boy cousins, girl cousins, adopted animal cousins—all were ready to do a cousin thing or two. For example, when Cousin Amy celebrated her ninth birthday, the McNeills searched the coffers for' some spendable cash to go toward a birthday present suitable for a party presentation. An idea came to Lily when she thought of the hours Amy and Lil played paper dolls together. They dressed and redressed those little cardboard creatures for days on end, but, sad to say, the dolls had no house to call their own.

Lily, the idea woman, rescued her old photo album with numbers and numbers of brown pages untouched by old snapshots. Perfect! From those pages came elegant furniture to place in a large box lid with the easily-recognized rooms partitioned by walls of album paper awaiting the usual household furnishings soon to come. The party was to be in two days. In the meantime, the house under construction even displayed a "Stairway to the Stars," beginning in the front hall and leading to . . . . ? On second thought, the architect and her young apprentice discontinued the stairway project.

The party was a success for Amy's Big 9, and the paper doll house was a hit, even though the dolls themselves were too heavy even to sit in one of the clever cutouts that had become a chair. Beds created the same problems. However, the little girls who played with the dolls conjured up degrees of imagined possibilities never having yet become a serious thought.

On a snowy Saturday, they were disgruntled because school was closed anyway. Lil imagined that the paper dolls slept "snug in their beds." Lily had a call from her new office suggesting she not try to walk to work that day. She was delighted but sensed her need to do something to please Lil. Anything. Because the child sneezed frequently that morning, the good mother decided to build a snow man under Lil's bedroom window in the hope of its bringing some enjoyment to the youngster who always preferred being outside—always outside—in the snow. But not that day. About the time Lily placed the smaller-but-taller mid-section on the large lower third of this icy creature she was forming, Amy's mother walked from across the street. Gingerly. She wore boots and a snug knitted toboggan and slushed through the snow to Lily's construction site. She was envious, she said, that she couldn't do likewise for Amy's pleasure, but maybe Lily would consider . . . ." Amy's taking a cold, too," she explained.

Shivering, Lily agreed, that "yes, she'd try to do that for Amy and 'our good relatives.'"

For the first time since their wedding day, all those years ago, Hubby oh-so-gently chastised his bride for promising two snow men in a single afternoon. He shuffled in to start supper; it was Lily's night to cook.

Cooking was not done by assignment. The chore just got worked out somehow. Even Lil was adept at frying cornbread and learning new recipes as she enjoyed her participation in good housekeeping.

A postscript here would have made much ado about plenty; however, one is due: In that era of blazing wood stoves in almost every kitchen, Lily and Neal had an uptown solution. Neal was a business man of high ideals and fairness. In his popular store downtown, he sold kerosene to many of his customers in the community. They used the clean-burning oil for certain types of living room heaters and for oil lamps in homes where electricity was unavailable. For cooking, it was a prize. Price of their modern kerosene-burning white enamel stove was the pleasure of the McNeills' very few appliances, and it was offered to Neal, the good merchant, at below cost. About kerosene, there's a story too good to miss—one that played in the store after school and/or on Saturdays. It was evident that parents in the surrounding villages—or those down town, for that matter, would send their children to the store with a nickel. The popular purchase was far-reaching: eight-year-old Toby O'Brian always searched for "Mr. Neal," who enjoyed to the full the boy's shopping list: "Mr. Neal, my mama tol' me to buy two cent worth o' kerosene and three cent worth o' broke-up candy." Neal loved Toby and all the children with the same request. They loved him, too, and how much of each product they could get for a split nickel.

From earlier days in the nicer house, but before the new kitchen stove, the electric refrigerator was queen. The surviving appliance was an old wooden box that required a block of ice each day if it did its job at all. Not on the first day, but no later than the second week, Lily and Neal moved the old box to the back porch until better days.

It was a time of dread for women, particularly if they had no method of keeping food, such as milk and butter, fresh. Lily, for example, sat at the kitchen table many a Saturday afternoon to enhance the margarine's appearance with those little packets of orangy-red powder that came with the block of oleo—which greatly resembled lard.

Before all the neighborhood cousins could sense that "spring is just around the corner," according to two blue birds exploring a bird house Neal had just nailed to a tree, school was already giving tests to determine highest averages in each grade. Lily was at work, of course, and Hubby had walked up to the neighborhood grocery for a loaf of whole wheat. As was his custom, he found friends drinking coffee and talking politics, so he joined the *kaffee-klatsch,* as well. He hadn't intended to stay long, but the Democrats' espousal of Roosevelt's second term was confident. Neal liked that; he had trouble tearing himself away.

Meanwhile, back at the community of cousins, meeting on the McNeills' front porch, Lil, Becky, Amy, and Millie each chose a rocking chair with cushion, an orange crush cola, and a serious attitude toward business at hand. In their youthful exuberance, they had an adult decision to make: what could they possibly contribute to the poor people about whom their folks were so concerned? A very brief silence burst forth into a more normal round of chatter. Lil had an idea: in the front hallway was a chest with a drawer that Mom had once left open long enough for Lil to rummage through it. Very carefully. The child had found some beautiful silky curtains, a light tan color, soft and smooth, but "Not useful anywhere in the house," she determined. "Perfect, though, for cutting down to size and making handkerchiefs for the poor!"

"Notion" carried.

Scissors were scarce, but in shifts of two girls at the time, geometric shapes began to appear—very few squares, but several elongated strips. They'd worry about precision later. Time was flying. Amy's mom was the first to call for her angel to come home for supper. Others followed suit. Lil knew Dad was back with the bread, and Mom would be coming in soon, for goo'ness sake. She hustled to toss the scraps back into the open drawer, which now wouldn't close. Too heavy. But Mom would be pleased; she knew she would.

Lily was *not* pleased. She checked the drawer's open status before she spied the geometric shapes which had apparently been recklessly tossed into the chest. The scissors were there, too. Lily's knees buckled when she dropped to the floor; she covered her face and cried. Her daughter hurried in to cry with her, each with her arms around the other. "Honey, what happened?" The puzzled mother couldn't understand.

"We just wanted to make handkerchiefs for the poor," Lil sobbed. "I thought you'd be proud." And I *am* proud, Darling. You, your friends, and I can make the handkerchiefs together. You won't mind if I help, will you?"

Once the shock had subsided, Lily removed from the drawer the other half of the pongee drapery which had hung in the bigger house for all her life with Neal until the finances slipped. "Fine Chinese silk won't do in this house anyway," she said to herself. Mother and daughter together closed the drawer but left the scissors behind so they'd have them handy Saturday afternoon.

In the meantime, the handkerchief project was delayed. The following verses made clear the fact that Lily lost her beloved spouse, and, Lil, her "precious daddy," as she referred to him ever after. Neal died of congestive heart failure in early March, 1941, too soon for spring to have shown its beauty or shared its warmth.

Our Lily spun in grief her heart unable to release
her spouse (best friend) and F.D.R. (her president) as well.
Her husband bled Depression wounds that Roosevelt bound up
too late to cure the anxious state o f living . . . having lost
his self worth and his business.

Her kindred came from far and near at her "Hubby's "death,
and once again they sat around a table-laden feast
the neighbors gave to show their love and hold this Lily fast
as she began a whole new life sans war, but oh! her spouse
whom she lost before her time.

They linger over grace at dinner, with granddad giving thanks
for baked brown hens, for grannie's yams and, oh yes, grannie, too.

The sister who's a punster's mum, but witty dad-in-law
says to sister, "Please pass the peas! For Peas and quiet, please!"
Then comes the bliss of laughter.

Too soon the laughter's hid by tears, but bear hugs save the day
as Ford engines moan and groan and bags fill up back seats.
Our Lily and her daughter, Lil, back in their empty house,
embrace as child and parent. They refigure travel miles
by future "reunitings."

Lily had resigned her job until plans could be made for her young daughter to be cared for after school. She, therefore, inherited the job of building a fire in the now-shared bedroom of mother and daughter, preparation for which included chopping wood, bringing both wood and coal inside, and, voila! lighting the fire. By the next fall, after Lil turned 12 in September, her mother showed her the art of chopping kindling with a small hatchet. Warmth became a joint effort, but Lily still heated a small blanket by the fire for Lil's feet to stay warm as she raced for her familiar old child's bed, then almost too small.

The jobless stretch for Lily was not easy, but as she declared often, "The Good Lord looks after us," and she believed the Grace-ful thanks prompting the comment that God saw a blessing for this mother-daughter duo in, of all things, the junior-senior prom at Sandy Hills High School. Lily and Lil could hardly believe the good fortune of some of the high school girls who needed—and whose families could afford—new evening dresses. Many moms remembered that Lily was an excellent seamstress, she having made Lil's school clothes that brought attention to the well-dressed child just entering her teens. The old Singer "Hubby" machine turned out some beautiful gowns for the local prom goers, often suggesting their origins came either from Rosemary Fashions downtown or maybe even one of the big stores in Raleigh. Lily's praises covered the neighborhoods, and the dress-maker's pocketbook kept the two as comfortable as they had ever thought possible.

Debbie Marks dressed in the most beautiful of all Lily's handmade gowns, was voted Queen of the Ball. In every way, she should have earned that vote: gown, hair style, grace, poise—they named her attributes. Lily, who was a chaperone at the prom—was also greeter, attention giver, hostess—took exactly four minutes from her official duties to compliment the Queen (AND take three minutes more to smile as she gazed at the dress adorning the young celebrity). "I made it!" said Lily to herself. The skirt, a net-layered rainbow of pastel colors— yellow, pale green, pink, lavender, and blue, was topped with a lighter blue-lined net bodice, suggesting the cloudless sky after a rain.

But soon Lily received a job offer she couldn't refuse. It was with a highly respected business on downtown Main, and, surprisingly, it offered more salary than she had ever made since her business course back when. The best reward for Lily was that she was able to rent an upstairs apartment in a lovely old house owned by good friends, and across the street from Laura, her forever friend in all the world. The distance from there to mid-town was four blocks. She was able to walk home for lunch, eat a bite, prepared by her responsible daughter, and return to her desk in an hour—unless, of course, a Camp Snyderman convoy was rumbling through her crossing corner.

As Lil aged beautifully, she no longer needed an at-home parent. Lily wanted to honor her for her gentle companionship with and respect for her mother and for her loving memory of her father, whom she adored for those 12 years he was with them. What would please Lil—Lily's very life, her friend, her pride and joy? "Yes. My pride and joy," she repeated. At that moment of reflection, Lily thought of the appreciative response that came from the six lovelies and their folks, who so liked the prom dresses. "I'm admitting to a rush of pride," she said to herself in the presence of the old Singer Sewing machine. From Hubby. "I'm going to Rosemary's tomorrow to buy my child a ready-made dress. She should certainly have at least one in her wardrobe during her lifetime." The adoring mother laughed because she loved her own idea.

Lil rushed to try on the brown and white checked dress with white cotton fringe stitched from the waist line over the shoulders, like suspenders. Smart! Stunning! (You had to see it.) She loved it, Lil did, but burst into tears when she saw the price tag read $6.50, embraced her mom, and graciously refused the gift. This time Lily cried, too, and swelled with whatever kind of pride that attacks mothers. She (also gently) insisted that Lil keep the gift. Both shed tears then. But not from sorrow.

The apartment was only half a block from the church held so dear to the family through the years. As the urge to keep adding to the story grows, only one more series of incidents needs reporting: Lily not only had worked her fingers to the bone at home, as Neal had repeated time after time, but "she was also on duty in God's house." It was true. Lily directed and taught in the Sunday school department for pre-schoolers on Sunday mornings, planned and directed the Sunday night youth program, presided over the women's mission group, and was church clerk—or record keeper, secularly speaking.

In the pre-school department with Lily, an enthusiastic young mother of two girls-the-right-age kept Sunday mornings interesting with personal experiences. But the children's entire group was, every week, memory-laden for years to come with the annual return of Susan Lawrence from a week-long statewide study camp for teachers of boys and girls who filled the little chairs and tables in their Sunday school classrooms.

Susan was enthusiastically watching the clock on the wall— the one on which the mechanical mouse ran up the length of the timepiece each time it struck "one" (every hour on the hour). Susan watched eagerly for Janet Rogers to come in because Janet was a little whirlwind who gave her teachers a beginning "guess what" to introduce every lesson. And that's precisely what Susan learned specifically at camp last week. She said to Lily, "One thing I know for sure, my friend, is you start the lesson at the very point of interest introduced by one child—or by the group. I can't wait to learn what I should say today. Oops! Here comes Janet!"

Janet burst into the room, sending the message that "At last! I'm so glad to be here finally!"

Susan Lawrence made a big to-do over Janet's entrance: "Well, Miss Rogers! I'm glad to see you! I was afraid . . . ."

Janet was giggling so that she could hardly speak, but was finally able to get out her excuse: "We're late today (giggle, giggle, and breathless), but my mommy couldn't find her girdle!" The other children enjoyed the funny excuse, too.

Susan, without a smile, turned to Lily and asked, "NOW what do I say first?"

Lily replied, "See me after class, and remember your topic," before she burst into laughter.

Susan, greatly relieved, was now living in her five minutes of uncontrollable pre-hysteria before she started the lesson on "forgiveness." After class, she said to Lily, "Well, nobody connected the lost girdle with the honor of forgiveness."

"They're children, dear one. There'll be another funny episode next Sunday. It's Jimmy Jamerson's birthday, and I'll have a cake for him," Lily reminded herself.

The following Sunday, the lesson majored on Jesus's visit to Mary and Martha. Lily said to Susan, "Their brother, Lazarus, you know, was a dear friend of Jesus."

During her lunch hour the very next day, Lily called up a new idea from the past: she went to the jewelry store, near her office, to visit Mr. Parsons, the jeweler, an idea person himself. She could always depend upon the sales staff there to think of a special—and free—way to illustrate the lesson to her children. Recalling a similar need a year or so ago, she asked if the store still kept china and silverware catalogs depicting colorful samples of merchandise printed on card stock.

"Of course, of course," Mrs. McNeill. "I was wondering when you'd need more," said the jeweler. Plates displayed in the big books were approximately the size of salad plates—perfect for the hostesses and hosts who would "serve Jesus" at Mary and Martha's. The cardboard eating utensils were nearly the same size as real-life sterling, for example. Lily left the store elated. Just what she'd need.

All week, with Lil's eagerness to help, mother and daughter cut out enough table settings "to feed New York," they teased.

On Saturday, Lily made the birthday cake for Jimmy. Early on Sunday, she took the realistic props across the street to the church and cleared away last week's art work left by the kiddies. At the last minute, she added six candles to the bithday cake, hiding the matches (knowing the exuberance of the children as she did.)

The small classroom tables were set beautifully by the well-supervised boys and girls, and the birthday cake was immensely enjoyed despite the inevitable sticky fingers. Jimmy, the birthday celebrant, was delighted to give away more than one piece of cake per friend—as long as he still had a slice each "for Mama and Daddy and their 'company.'"

Two days later, Jimmy's mother called Lily to thank her for "all the excitement my boy enjoyed on Sunday."

The next day, Mr. Jamerson stopped by the office and asked for Lily. They greeted each other warmly, and Mr. Jamerson was exceedingly cordial. He said, "Mrs. McNeill, we've had more fun over Jimmy's visitor Sunday."

"Oh?" Lily was puzzled.

"Sure did," said Mr. Jamerson. "The minute Jim got in the car to go home, he said, "Daddy, Jesus is comin' to town today! . . . and, Mrs. McNeill, the sweet thing about it was he brought my wife and me a piece of your delicious cake, and one to save for Jesus. And then he related to us the story you told the class about Jesus visiting Mary and Martha. He understood the whole thing—except about how Jesus was coming to Sandy Hills. I just wanted you to know how nice it is that he understands much but gets a little confused at age six. Thank you so much. I'm highly pleased with his teachers."

"Thank YOU, Mr Jamerson." Lily was a little choked up for her report to Susan.

POSTSCRIPT: According to the legal records of the Sandy Hills Court House, "The Closest LILY" was born September 10, 1894 and died on March 13, 1994 at age 99.

To all the lilies who touched our lives in the first half of the 20th century, and to all who "toil and spin" with comparable energy today:

A Tribute

The stories of some lilies end, but memories abide.

Remember, if you will, the struggles, stresses, fears of years

that may have slowed them in their toil, but still they cited lights

of service living in their souls. How bright the lights, we ask?

BRIGHT AS LOVE AND DIGNITY!

Study this imagined portrait: look long into each face

in the event you see someone who "toiled" and "spun" for you.

Her image now may offer you a memory long lost:

(Her record's in the Registry of Heaven's Treasured Names.)

YOU WOULDN'T WANT TO MISS HER.

Illustration lit by life calls on brush strokes to sustain

compassion, faith, and lasting joy for each eternal guest.

But how will Lilies rest at last, there in the mansion's rooms?

They might consider the lilies God planted in the fields . . .

. . . or themselves!

(He blessed their work)

Miss B's Front Porch "Farm" was Her Neighborhood in 1926

Georgia Bailey churned vigorously on Monday and Thursday mornings in the shade of her old familiar front porch—cooler than her indoor rooms, granted, but also a much warmer atmosphere for personal contact with passersby. Interestingly, some neighbors knew her daily routine and calculated which days would interest them. For example, walkers on Mondays and Thursdays were quite aware of the to-die-for butter molds that "Miss B" was able to coax out of the chum in just the right shape. "Country butter," they called it gratefully, as they prided themselves for all they'd done toward oleomargarine replacement.

Each Tuesday, Wednesday, and Friday, "Miss B" again worked on her front porch "farm," shucking corn and shelling peas, snapping beans, peeling and slicing enough apples for pies as well as a good wintertime stock of canned sauce in her pantry. On some Saturday mornings, she forsook the porch to bake lemon meringue pies in the summer-time temperatures of her den of delight—her kitchen. According to her practice, she set each pie on a window sill to cool. She watched over those beauties as closely as a hen would keep an eye on her biddies; however, on one of those very warm days in her very warm kitchen, she created only one pie. But, lo! it was beautiful.

"Indeed, this is the perfect model of my entire pie career!" She congratulated herself that Saturday, rest assured. As she placed the pie in the window, admiring it without ceasing, she spied a tiny lady bug resting on the screen. She liked lady bugs, so she was very careful in leaning over the sill to thump the tiny red and black creature off its resting place before she started to spread peanut butter and jelly sandwiches for her children and their cousins who were playing outside.

"Whew! Lunch time already," she reminded herself.

"And, oh my, who's that knocking on the back door?" It was Adam, the ice man. "Adam, welcome! You brought enough ice to keep us cool 'til Monday. Right?"

"Sure did, Miss B. "I'll be back Monday mornin'!"

*"The ice man cometh" every day to keep the ice box fed
and often brings inside the drink that milkman fed the porch.
Other Lilies still hold on to Frigidaires with ice trays which also freeze
fresh peach ice cream that never ever melts—
unless, of course, it's August.*

Miss B and the talkative old black man with a stunning white beard chatted a bit about the new preacher at his church-AME Zion—when she thought of still-unmade sandwiches for the kiddies. So back inside she scurried just as she heard Adam commanding the mules to move on with the ice haul for the day: "Giddy-up thar, you mules!"

But the pie heroine gasped upon returning to her kitchen to find that the pie-award-of-the century had lost its crowning glory. "Well," she bellowed, hands on hips, "Where in the world did my beauty go? WHERE?"

Her choice remarks echoing through the rear of the house, she dashed to the front door. "Lou! Tee! Suz! Johnny! Get in the house this minute!" The youngsters paused just long enough to ask questions with their eyebrows before bursting through the kitchen door.

"Anything wrong, Mama?" asked Tee.

Miss B could only answer with a question: "Who, Tee, WHO has been into my pie?"

"Not me," declared Johnny.

"Not I, Johnny," the former teacher corrected her nephew.
"Me neither," returned Johnny, wide-eyed.

A little shaky from the tone of their favorite story teller, Tee
and Suz acquitted themselves by quoting a fresh-off-thewires
popular denial—with hands over their hearts: "Cross my heart
and hope to . . . ."

The story teller, same tone, nipped that clandestine move in
the bud: "We don't use that remark in this house, girls. Ever."

Finally, eight-year-old Lou, the little helper, said, "There it is,
Mama! The meringue! And, look. Aw . . . there's a little tiny lady
bug on it." All eyes followed Lou's pointing finger to just below
the waistline of Miss B's apron.

After following Lou's helpful directions, Miss B collapsed
in a chair laughing convulsively. The children laughed too,
before they even got the joke. They would savor the meringue
story forever because it was so typical of Mama (Miss B to the
cousins) to be doing four things at once, such as searching for
a missing meringue, talking church with the ice man, rescuing
a lady bug, and serving a sandwich lunch to six of her favorite
children. Each child also received a bear hug and, of course,
according to Johnny, "a piece of lemon pie without no icing on
it at all."

But Johnny wasn't quite ready to call it a day. After lunch, he
and Miss B sat on the front steps for a time to watch the other
children ride their horses, which were usually made from apple
tree limbs.

Johnny seemed restless. Finally, he asked the big question:
"Miss B., what time is it?"

"Well, I don't know, son; I don't have a watch, but the
beautiful sunshine tells me it's almost one o'clock."

"Oh," said Johnny.

"What's on your mind, dear? You're one of my favorite
nephews in the whole world, and I don't want you to be shy
around me. Would you like for me to get you an apple branch
that would be a good horse for you to ride with your cousins?"

"No'm. I guess I was just thinkin' you go to the movies a lot
on Saturday to the double features. I was hopin' you would go

today so I could come to your house tomorrow afternoon and hear some of the good stories you tell about them horse riders 'n' all."

"Tell you what, Johnny," started the story teller's famous magic words, "You go ask your mama if you can go with me to the second movie . . . we'll have to hurry . . . tell her I've got a dime to pay your way . . . if they even charge you . . . I'll meet you at the corner . . . wear your cowboy hat . . . run now."

"I love you, Miss B." he yelled as he tripped over his untied shoe lace.

"And then we can both tell the front porch boys and girls what all we saw!" Typical. She was as excited as he.

1927

Josie Names Lovely Ladies of the Coop

In uncertain financial times, the back porch was invariably useful to the family whose home was so fortunately constructed. For one thing, it was usually screened to discourage the busy fly and mosquito wars' easy access to the summer battlefield.

The family of Josephine and William fortunately lived at town's edge on land they were able to retain in those dreadful times; how they longed for continued ownership. William, a farmer, with his tenants who lived nearby, grew vegetables and tended a few animals—a cow, four dogs, two cats, and a plethora of hens (generous egg producers), plus a few roosters.

Corn was king, with beans, squash, turnips, cabbage, carrots, eggplant, potatoes, yams, and cucumbers being subjects in the royal order. Melons and fruit trees boosted the finances.

On the back porch near the kitchen door, the ice box stood against the rear wall of the peeling yellow house paint. While the location of the ice was readily accessible, the length of life for the frozen block depended upon the summer's heat.

At the opposite end of the porch, a pile of firewood, drying after tree-cutting in the early spring, was ready for fall and winter's heat but would likely be depleted by November's end. An old manual sewing machine competed with other useful products, as did four boys' bicycles plus a small doll house for small girls.

But the grace of the back porch was a large table covered in blue and white oil cloth (forerunner of plastic?) with 16 matching chairs—two at each end and six on either side. The family, well-blessed with relatives nearby, used most of the chairs for supper on any cool of the evening. But sometimes the table was set and ready for the harvesters who came on appointed days for a breakfast of fried chicken, grits, hot biscuits, and baked apples, made more palatable (if anyone could desire more palatability) by strong hot coffee, usually black, and always enough. On those mornings, Josie (short for Josephine) would arise at 4:00 a.m. to have the chicken done and biscuits coming out of the oven when the "guests" arrived at 6.00.

With young boys in the family, Josie and William never knew what one would decide to say that early in the morning about his baked apples. Or something. That morning, Billy, 12, revealed the story he told in his fourth grade class about some interesting things you have to do to have a delicious chicken breakfast. One of the harvesters joined the discussion: "I bet your dad does all the hard stuff, and your mom does the frying."

Before Billy could answer, his father jumped in. He seemed a little unhappy to say, "Uh, no, Claude. I can't stomach all that. Josie's always my right hand when it comes to gettin' chickens ready to cook . . . 'n' cookin' 'em, too, I reckon."

Josie was sometimes reluctant to recall preparing one of those early breakfasts. She began on the previous morning by capturing three of the hens (all bearing female names), slaughtering them in the kindest way, undressing them, and groaning at the sight of those tiny pin feathers still left; therefore, with her three captives in tow, she hastened to the kitchen, where the wood stove blazed and matches were handy. As always, Josie brushed a tear from her cheek as she singed the remaining stubble away and placed the hens in cold water for the sake of freshness.

She wept at recalling the tender names she had awarded the little ladies of the coop—Lucille, Elvira, and Tish—as well as their affection toward her. Josie ate no chicken that morning nor had she since christening Rosie, Lula, Mary

Margaret, and Katrina, the first four occupants of the hens' dormitory in 1923.

"Watch it, Billy," said Dad. "Let's don't talk about who does the hard stuff to get chickens ready to be cooked. Okay?"

Welcome to Wash Day

Monday, October 4, 1937

They soak their Monday's laundry in hot, steamy lye-soap suds,
prelude to bleach and clothes-line-dry, sun-blessed and smelling clean.
No rest for toiling Lilies. See? They know what comes next day!
We wonder if they ever dream of no-press cotton blends?
Too fanciful an image?

Summer or not, Ethel had to have that fire under the old iron pot blazing hot for wash day. How comfortable she was last night, knowing that tomorrow was the first Monday in October—on the cusp of cold weather but not quite there yet. The black iron wash pot had been in place for decades, or so it seemed. It rested authoritatively over the hole dug underneath, where they lit the fire every Monday. Sometimes it would catch on the first lighting, sometimes on the fourth or fifth. Much depended on how dry the wood was and how much kindling had been laid in a wash-day design (intermingled) with other fuels, such as coal, oak branches, and yesterday's loosely-rolled bi-weekly journal. The big pot was king down in the old horse cart path. Close to it stood a sizeable wash board in case of need for hearty scrubbing.

Certain traditions remained in effect. Ethel was always in charge. At 86, old as she was, she was spry in the wash day mode, and never had her reputation been tarnished. Today, she hollered clear across the fences where the pole beans flourished: "Jackson, bring me them overhalls off the line. No! Them that never got moved inside all last week. I got to wash 'em again." With a barely audible rumble boiling up through her hoarseness, she'd add a comment, not always in earshot, but all in the wash-pot lineup knew what she meant about clean clothes being left on the line all week.

Two tin wash tubs nearby were ready to receive hot water, bucket by bucket, hour by hour, from the wood stove in the kitchen. Always fresh, the steamy elixir was plentiful for more delicate laundry than that for which the old iron tub would qualify: table cloths, crocheted antimacassars for chair backs and arms, men's good shirts, women's undergarments and outerwear, as well, top and bottom sheets from three beds one week and from two the next. (Ethel carefully recorded which beds were assigned to which schedule.) But both sheets of Swanee's tiny bed were washed each week.

Even then, it was old news that dipping whites in bluing kept them from turning yellow; and, lo, it was true. They were whiter than ever in each dipping.

Equipment was a major topic of conversation on October Monday. It was as if the participants were more determined to do what they should be doing all day. LeRoy Ellis, a faithful member of the crew, brought two new wash boards, sturdy, but smaller than the old grandfather board up by the iron pot.

LeRoy had done a study and reported that this size was more useful than some large ones even when the strong soap failed to remove a spot by scrubbing—by hand and skinned knuckles. These new mobile boards were known for "best in show" after a garment's inaugural cleansing.

Last but not least, tobacco sticks became progressively important for lifting clean laundry from the tubs. Given the width of the sticks, some women found it difficult not only to handle the sticks but also to add soaking wet wash to the weight and shape of them. Many of the men "on call" answered with help.

But clothes claimed drying habits of their own. And why not? Of the five beds in the house, only one was smaller than regular size. At that season, the litte one was the eight-hour night place for Swanee, but she likely wouldn't own it long. Her aunt, Julia Lee, might be claiming it in five weeks when she'd have her baby—could be a little boy, if its father-to-be could choose the gender.

Widely believed in that community of kin and friends was that if Julia's husband, Mack, chose, the baby would be Mack, III. It was more a guess than a belief of both mother-and father-to-be. Both counted the weeks until she could be repainting the child's bed, anyway. When the family asked her the proposed new color, she'd likely answer, "Well, whatever color Mack wants it to be." (Guess)

When Mack fielded the same question, he also gave his identical response: "Well, it depends on the Lord, Who creates babies, what gender He gives ours, and what would make Julia happy, but I tell you right now, she wants a girl (belief), so I'd say just leave the bed pink. And for the record, I'd love either— boy or girl—and so would Julia. I know that."

"Can't just leave the bed pink," Julia declared. "My word, Swanee's slept in it four years now. Not pink no more. Sort of grayish. I want my bsby to start out in a pretty new bed made of hickory wood—dainty but sturdy branches—like, you know, to suit an adorable baby." Mack squirmed. He thought Julia was going to cry right there in front of everybody.

But Fred, Swanee's dad, Monty's husband, and Mack's older brother, spoke up and said just the right thing: "Hey, Mack, how come I don't meet you down at Hickory Ridge next, say, next Wednesday, and we buy enough hickory branches and logs for the little one you and Jule will have? You know, for what seems right for a baby? Then you and me can make it a beautiful bed."

Mack looked greatly relieved and said, "Fred, you've done come up with it now. You're on track, for sure, good buddy. And Mr. Choplin don't charge much money. I think we can do that."

But why was Julia just standing there smiling? (Guess: She liked what she heard from Mack—new bed for new baby!)

Mack saw the smile and found it inviting. He walked toward her and she ran to embrace him. "Thank you, dear one, I . . . Wait, Mack. Who is that little beauty toddling down the path?"

"Well, little beauty, where did you come from? Jule, I believe it's Swanee. Are you Swanee?" He stooped to lift her, jerking off his heavy shirt: too warm for layers, he had decided.

The child was then lifting her arms up to him, and he accepted her invitation, held her tight for a moment against his clean white undersdhirt. Julia was beaming. "What a little beauty," she said to herself. Swanee's hair was golden—the color of last night's moon. Julia hurried over to Mack to join the triple embrace.

Swanee was delighted and squealed in her own native tongue to let them know she recognized them.

"Life don't get no better'n this, Jule," declared the husband with such meaning that she had to brush away a tear from her cheek.

"Yes" was all she could think of to say.

Mack had just set the toddler back on the path when he heard Ethel's raspy voice calling, "Mack? MACK?"

"I heard ya, Grandma Ethel," he hollered as loudly as she had.

By the time both sides were laughing, Ethel said, "I don't want to nag you, boy, but if you and somebody you choose to help don't soon drag that wringer over near the action, our laundry won't get dry 'til Wednesday. We'd be in a pickle for sure, we would." Ethel had become a pretty no-nonsense accuser when it came to telling her grandson, Mack, what to do when, and how to do it.

"Be there with wringer in five minutes, Grandma. Meet you at the big wash pot." Old age might have something to do with her mood, but for sure, he thought, it was more than likely wash day.

Meanwhile, Julia had perched on the front porch bannister to do a little thinking about her condition. "Five more weeks," she said out loud. Her sister-in-law, Monty, Swanee's young mama, was on the other side of the porch hand sewing something for that little darlin' of a four-year-old.

"Hey, Monty," Julia offered, as she walked across the wide flooring toward her sister-in-law.

"Oh, Julia. Sorry. I'm so wrapped up in making some decent clothes for Swanee that I hardly know where I am." sighed Monty. You know, Julia, sewing is such a chore to me. I can't do it. I can't stand it. But in all the time I've lived here, I've never seen a woman at a sewing machine, I've never seen one basting a seam from her lap, I've never seen one even . . . even crocheting. Where are all the smart women who sew?'

"You ever been in our bedroom, Monty?"

"No I haven't. I think of them as the only private places we have. Am I wrong, Julia?"

"Well, if you look into ours any night from, say, 7:00-10:00, you just might see something you'd like. Remember: Hey! stop in tonight. Please, Monty, say yes. And let me take that dress you were about to toss. Could I try something?"

"Take it and toss it, by all means," said Monty.

"No. I'll tell you this, though. If you'll let me take this dress you're making for Swanee, I promise she'll have a new one by noon tomorrow."

"Julia, you can't be serious, can you?" Monty had to know.

"And a bit further, if I'm not intruding, you say you have some more material for her clothes? I'll be delighted to finish up another two or three in as many days. Am I being too forward, Monty?"

Monty burst into tears. "Julia, what can I say? I've got material—if you can call flour sacks and feed sacks material—how can I thank you? How could I pay you? How do we deserve your generosity?" She wept again.

Julia, her arm around Monty's shoulder and eager to speak, said, "Thank me? be my friend. Pay me? for what I want to do more than anything? Deserve? Let me ask you how I can deserve you and Swanee and Fred? Tell you the truth, Monty, I've always wanted our families to be close We are kin, you know. Now with my little one on the way, maybe . . . ."

They open wide their windows at the setting of the sun
to let October breezes in, watch curtains' nightly dance.
The old machine begins to stitch as it is wont to do
—making straight the seams that Lily conspires each time to sew
on her trusty old Singer.

The sisters-in-law sang four lines of "Happy Wash Day to You" to
the tune of "Happy Birthday"—Julia sang soprano and Monty sang
alto.

1937

The Irony of Press Day

"Rise and shine, beautiful bride," were the first words of Press Day, October 5, 1937, to reach the ears of Lulu, the new wife of Prescott, son of the long-established Mumford clan so well regarded in their small community of Sandstone Way. Lulu jumped, pulled the pillow over her pretty face, covering her short black hair (with bangs), and stayed perfectly still for as long as Scotty, her groom, would allow.

"What? Did I frighten you, Sweetie?" he inquired softly. "Oh, Scotty, of course you didn't scare me. It was what you implied," she answered.

"Was it 'rise and shine' or 'beautiful bride?'" he teased.

"Neither, Honey, it was all the implications of today. You know how I am about new situations and 'entertaining strangers unawares.' By then, she was returning his warm embrace.

"Oh, yes, of course. Press Day." He stood away from her just arms' length and whispered, "But breakfast is under way in five minutes."

"You go," she urged. "Just let me get presentable." "But . . . ," he started.

"No I'm not either but soon will be. See you at the table." Each threw the other that proverbial early morning kiss.

Lulu waited outside the dining room door until she heard Daddy Mumford's closing, "in Whose name we pray. Amen."

For a reason she did not identify, she suddenly felt warm and included. "What a treat," she said to herself at the same time she apologized to the family for missing Grace.

But, of course, Dad also apologized for starting without her.

"Coffee, Lulu?" Mary Ellen, the older sister inquired, as she poured a generous cupful without a reply.

Mama Mumford was in a talkative mood at breakfast, but not currently into the future events of the day. A touch here and there of yesterday's wash marathon seemed to be on her mind as she recalled one such event of bygone months when the weather was not suited for drying, and the family's only choice was to hunker down under wet sheets for two days before enough fires in the house took care of dripping bed clothes as well as socks, underwear, and men's good shirts. Then she addressed Lulu: "I think I had one of those spells you say you have — you know — so stressful . . . ."

"The word for me, Mother Mumford, is 'anxiety.' Terrible!"

"But your anxiety is better now, Lulu"? Mary Ellen wanted to hear. "If it is, I want to know how to treat mine!"

"How'd you get on at church Sunday?" Mother Mumford's curiosity bounded. "I can guess that before you got to a pew, somebody, said, 'You from around here?'"

Lulu immediately began to back away from the anxiety, and she succeeded by laughing (although she didn't think it funny.) "Interesting you should have guessed that question, Mother. It was the very first one addressed to me . . . ."

"And I know some more, too: 'Where you from?' 'Are ya'll gonna live with the Mumfords?' 'Does Scotty have a job yet?'

'Who's your daddy?'" Mrs. Mumford paused.

Lulu jumped in. Quite unexpectedly, she commanded the entire attention span at the table when she offered, "But I wanted to talk about Tuesday, October today — the very day after wash day. I might venture the studied opinion that 'Today might be one of the more *pressing* days of our lives together, and I don't mean to be *ironic.*'" Perhaps for the first time in her young life, Lulu brought the house down, so to speak. Scotty beamed. His family laughed on and on and then some. Lulu blushed and loved being funny: funny, maybe, for the first time ever.

Mother Mumford murmured under her breath: "Thanks for our first good laugh from the bride. Hope more's to come." Of course, Lulu heard every syllable; her delight soared.

"Ten-thirty already?" asked somebody in the kitchen, where the wood stove was doing its job, keeping irons of one design or another ready for pressing; a fireplace in the dining room, just now heating up where three small ironing boards can take care of clothes for children; and four large boards on the back porch, where irons heated in the kitchen can stand short pauses to reach the porch in time for a touch-up if not more.

"Hey, Mama, do we have any of those cardboard or even palm fans like the church uses? We don't? Do you think it would be O.K. if we borrowed a few? We'll take 'em back before Sunday. Scotty said he'd run get 'em. It's hot in this house!"

Some cardboard fans at a general store down the road did the trick. When Scotty returned with four fans, he had news. He had run into a neighbor—if you call five miles away your neighborhood—and could hardly wait to invite her to use one of the ironing boards in the kitchen. All such essentials were taken at her house over in the next county. "She was Julia—the wife of Macon Thomas. He was driving his dad's old Ford, and Julia was with him just because she had no board to iron on at their house. All the boards—and irons, too—were being used. And you know what I did? I invited 'em to come here this afternoon and iron on that small board in the kitchen—the one like Lulu's using. Now Julia's got a reputation about ironing children's clothes, so she's going to bring some over here and get Lulu to help her. I don't think it'll take long." He hardly finished his story before Julia knocked on the front door.

Lulu answered the knock. "Oh, it's Julia—my pew mate from church last Sunday. I'm glad to get to know you better. I told the family how nice you were to me. Thank you."

"Thank you, Lu. It is Lu, isn't it?" Julia looked uncertain. "It's Lu if you want it to be, Julia. The family members double the syllables and call me Lulu. Either is fine with me." "Lulu it will be," assured Julia as she turned to greet the still unknowns—all waiting in line.

As she met the group, Julia breathed deeply and said, "Your house smells delicious. That steam from the irons and the fires combined just makes me want to enjoy the odor—is it cedar? or pine? Whatever, it is, it's perfume."

Lunch served on outside picnic tables was delicious—"Mother-Made," said Dad Mumford to the skeptical family and visitors. "Daddy-Made," corrected his wife. "Dad and the sons did the honors. Applause, everyone!" Still-warm chicken roasted outside, cold potato salad (with dill), deviled eggs, home-grown baked squash with brown sugar, and pie made from apples from the trees next door and baked by Clarice, who lives there. Thanks to good neighbors.

The presiding officer, Mother Mumford requested time for an announcement or two before they adjourned to their pressing stations. "Because so much time hastened by in our understanding of what to do and how to do it, we lost a little. But no problem, I assure you. The fires are just right, says my husband, and the irons are heating well. I'm asking my new daughter, Lulu, and her new friend, Julia, to work together on the small boards with the smaller irons to focus on the children's clothes. Julia, a starch expert, drove from Stony Point in the family Ford to give us some tips on finishing little girls' dresses. So Julia, would you tell us the process? Can't wait to see how you'd prepare the little dress for ironing. We hid the one you finished just last night, but it's high time we introduced it. Are you ready, Julia? And welcome."

"Thanks, Mrs. Mumford."

Julia held in her hand a wad of wet material, which she twisted until the dripping almost stopped. She then placed it in a pan of well-mixed "starchy starch," she explained, without indicating the brand. The next step was to move the dress container to a nearby table for a few minutes.

Lulu, at the next ironing board and table, followed Julia's every move with a new dress for the six-year-old niece, whom she met just last week. Hers was once a flour sack. It had been dipped in its own pan of starch. Since she was not acquainted with the details of the style and pattern, she chose not to describe the product, but only to fulfill her assigned duties.

Julia continued narrating both demonstrations. She explained, "I made this dress from a flour sack, too. The little angel, Swanee, is my niece, whom I adore. The pale pink flowers reminded me of her, so I tried to do my best to design a short dress with full skirt and little puffed sleeves. I kept the bodice dainty—tucked *and* smocked, with the smocking in pink. The sash that attaches to each side seam, ties in the back." Enough explaining, she must have decided, so she retrieved the soaked-in-starch dress and, with both hands, she squeezed the liquid from the tiny wad of pink and white material. That done, she moved to another container and splashed generously with clear water the object of the moment.

Lulu hastily retrieved her pan of starch from the nearby table, too. She seemed very relaxed, which surprised her family. And herself. Obviously, she had paid close attention; she didn't miss a single point of Julia's finely tuned presentation. She chose, however, to reassure herself at this crucial point: "Julia, I assume your next step is the ironing itself."

"You're exactly right, Lulu. Seems to me it's time for close communion. Why don't you move over here with me and we'll figure this out together." Lulu was ready to do just that, as soon as she gathered her show and tell equipment.

Then came the choice of irons: Of the several on display, a few antiques had already been retired to door stop duty in some old homes a bit older than the houses of that day. The two demonstrators said later that they were tempted to ask for the irons they used that afternoon to keep as souvenirs; however, they agreed that the memories of the day would be enough, and irons would be necessary for Press Days far into the future.

Some of them were still being heated in less advanced ways than by electricity; for one thing, not enough outlets were available yet throughout the house. Also, it took a while to collect them for the needs of just one day a week.

Lulu ironed first (to get it done quickly). But at her insistence, she and Julia would be shoulder to shoulder throughout the press "competition." Her handmade sample was somewhat a copy of style and fit that Julia had sewed for Swanee. The onlookers were neither close nor quiet enough to notice similarities in the dresses.

Lulu's very small flat iron, heated on an anvil-like device that came from the nearby wood stove, moved smoothly along the skirt but more slowly on the short sleeves and tiny buttons on the blouse. The bubble of steam created soft sizzles and pleasant odors to the end, and the new bride, new family member, and new friend took a bow.

Julia's iron cord ran all the way up to the socket in the ceiling. It danced along to wherever she moved. Julia, a slightly more polished seamstress, seemed a bit less concerned as to whether she removed every wrinkle, but the way she twisted and fluffed her product turned all senses of wonder toward perfection.

During the applause, the two young women took their bows, holding hands, smiling widely, and mouthing "thank you."

Mrs. Mumford put a clean sheet over one of the tables at the front, and gave the young artists a nod. Each picked up her own creative result and, and . . . Yes!

Each stood her starched dress on the new table, *and each dress stood alone!* For about three seconds, all was silent, but after the fourth: Press Day Pandemonium.

The two young heroines taking bows had invaded the tradition.

1938

Miss Nettie and Her Corsetiere(s)

Her persona in 1938 was as familiar to her community as if she, forever after, starred in a role at the local playhouse—even though there had never been a local playhouse. Actually, the widely known "drama star" lived in her family's old home place. Admittedly, it reminded observers of a stage play in progress; however, only Miss Nettie kept the perception alive—even as the town's admirers noticed and greatly appreciated her sometimes mysterious moves.

That she managed a peaceful countenance and steady analogous poise through the tragedies befalling her close-knit family was an anomaly to the townspeople who knew her well—or not so well. What a valiant response she felt called upon to make as the 1918 flu pandemic claimed the lives of both her father and younger sister. But tragedy continued; at about the time World War I was ending, her brother-in-law never made it home from his first wartime service, although he had planned a military career from his high school years. But these events were two decades past, only to be revisited ten years later by an old age happenstance that left Miss Nettie bereft of her mother as well. She and her cats, Melinda and Martha, may have wept in the dark nights of loneliness, but her days showed mostly her constant gratitude for the past and her cats' pleas for yet another serving of leftover delights from her table.

Always well groomed, she was a tall, seventy-five-ish elegant woman who was hesitant to walk to her side-of-the-road mailbox without wearing hose and a touch-up with her face cream, although powder wasn't necessary, so declared the cold cream advertisements. Her hair, always set in the style she chose for the day, was not yet completely white, but almost. And her once obviously-expensive garments added a touch of good taste for that day's style or for the fashions of five years earlier. Or maybe later. But her sense of personhood came not from fashion but rather from her family's belief that "Cleanliness is next to Godliness." And her devotion to work was born in a sense of service, so said her admirers who had seen her life's work defined by gardening in her sizeable acreage for growing edibles.

They spin in fields of blue larkspur and crocheted
Queen Anne's lace
or acres white with cotton bolls far as the eye can see.
They watch their peaches ripen, their tomatoes turning red,
sly kudzu creeping closer to the melon vines out back
as summer does its bidding.

"Aye, there's the rub!" The common town talk centered on the knowledge that Miss Nettie (always the excellent performer) had a visitor once a month in the person of her corsetiere, who had befriended her. Only once did the new friend find her hostess in tears rather than in her garden at work, but the visitor shed a tear, as well, on learning that it was the birthday anniversary of Miss Nettie's mother. After a brief tribute to the deceased, the lone daughter immediately regained her composure, so delighted was she to see Miss Morrison, the "best in all of corsetry," according to the guest's professional reputation.

The two got down to business at the showing of a new and imposing "under garment," as both women called it, that covered a customer to the full extent of the law requiring that corsets shape, yet do no damage to female frames. (As to those onlookers who knew only *of* Miss Nettie, she became the "corset lady." But after seeing her bend from the waist to pluck a basket of strawberries, for example, the onlookers continued their current discussion as to how the older woman could force her torso to accommodate weeding and plucking—to say nothing of stooping to gather eggs from generous hens?)

The few children left in the woman's life were the young girls next door who adored their elder "Aunt Nettie," although as far as anyone knew, she was no one's aunt at all. Suffice it to say, she would never have dressed without the three "little nieces," as she called the girls, and for whom she was thankful that they were out of school for much of the growing season and could help her significantly as her garden matured. The corset became defiant in the warmest weather, of course, and she instructed the girls as to where to hold their tiny fingers tight while she laced up as rigidly as her breathing allowed.

Miss Nettie worked inside on rainy days, of course, also during the darkest hours when she needed to can, cook, shell limas, or make pickles. In her prolific garden, one of the most treasured forms of produce was melons, particularly watermelons and cantaloupes (her preferred name for what some friends called muskmelons). She never forgot her close neighbors on warm, starry nights when she served spring-cooled watermelons from her picnic table on the grassy lawn near the back steps. Sometimes, with help from her guests, she would slice seven or eight of the ripest carriers of that nectar that oozed from every bite of the rare melon meat.

There was more than hospitality in the mind of Miss Nettie as she organized the watermelon gala; she also knew how many of the melons' rinds her partying friends would discard on the grass as they ate. She simply must clean up the mess? No. She simply must gather up the rind remnants for extreme cleaning before cutting them into small pieces for pickling. For that job, she got her old brogans from the back porch closet so she wouldn't ruin her everyday shoes in the process. "Rind gets mushy," she reminded the girls who came to help her lace her corset.

At her watermelon party, the guests couldn't stop talking about the pickles. "Pickling"? they asked. "Watermelon rind pickles? Incredible," they said, and, remembering the comments, Miss Nettie discontinued the party until the day before Thanksgiving. For that afternoon, she invited the neighbors to return to her spotless pantry to see a rainbow of colorful jellies, pickled rinds, sunny canned fruit, and fig preserves.

Wilson and Kate from next door had already planned to ask the big question: "Miss Nettie, Kate and I admire you so much and think often about all the curtsying, bowing, and bending you do in your work, as well as your church and social life. Could you let us in on your secret? You know, how can you bend so easily after our girls help you lace up every morning?"

Kate added, "Please don't be offended, dear. We're just wondering how you always move so freely."

Miss Nettie cackled, her hand over her mouth. Yet, smiling, she said, "Kate, wondering is a lot harder than bending. So I'm glad you and Wilson asked. It's just practice, dear, just practice. Besides, I have to wear something tight to hold in my grief at the tragic losses of my precious family through the years."

Well! They never thought of that. But it would be true of Miss Nettie, wouldn't it?

Before her guests left on that Thanksgiving eve, she gave each a jar of her homemade watermelon rind pickles. "They go well with turkey," said Miss Nettie as she bowed from the waist in a cordial, yet dramatic, farewell gesture.

The crowd roared with delight. But little did Nettie know that Kate and Wilson and their three young daughters (the junior corsetieres) had already set an extra plate at the table for her—and one for Miss Morrison, the professional corsetiere—for tomorrow's Thanksgiving dinner.

1941

Molly's *a Cappella* Choir Sings in the Trees

"Mama Molly," was the name bestowed upon Molly McCrary by her six children: Marianne, Trish, Julie, Cindy, Tark, and Terry of 4605 Piney Paths in Sandy Hills. Molly's husband, Judd, called her by his own pet name: "Molly Love."

The Molly of note was a music teacher for the entire elementary school system of the county. Piano lessons were her forte, but she also played and taught flute, violin, clarinet, organ, and handbells. Ordinarily, she taught in her own studio wing at the large elementary school in town but occasionally visited the smaller surrounding districts. Greatly respected as a teacher, as a musician, and as a talented woman, she easily developed lasting relationships. Her five-year-old twin son Tark observed, "Mama Molly likes everybody, but she loves little people like me 'all the morether.'" After Tark invented the word "morether," the world of words lit up for him and his twin brother, Terry, until they reached the age of six—"going on thirteen," offered their sister, Marianne, twelve.

Major Judson W. McCrary was commissioned upon his graduation from the Citadel in Charleston and had long ago developed an admiration for the military. "He will likely be deployed to Europe as unrest builds there and in other vulnerable spots around the globe," said Molly to no one in particular. She tried not to think that "worries come in bunches," but the phrase wouldn't leave her mind. "Her mantra?" She questioned herself.

A sharp decrease in the number of some of her very best students, who had long taken private Saturday piano lessons, increased her concerns. How would she manage without the Saturday's lessons? How would she feed, clothe, and educate six youngsters, all, of whom, were twelve and under? "Oh, God, what happened to our world? Where was that *agape* love for which we had so sincerely hungered?"

At that moment of Molly's loneliness, Judd walked in, having been given a two-week furlough from Fort Bragg before he was to report to the Pentagon for a hush-hush meeting for August 12-19. Not having seen him in a week, she threw her arms around him, shedding tears that surprised him.

"Honey, what is it? Are you upset about something specific? Oh, you've missed me. How sweet of you!"

"I have missed you, of course, and, Judd, I'm scared."

"I am, too, Molly Love. Let's make a pact to face the future with what happens then and not be frightened now. By the way, what's this I've heard about your Saturday piano lessons?"

"Money's too scarce. I've had six of eight call just last week to say they can't afford them any longer. And, you know, I miss those lessons dreadfully. Miss Kitty had always sat on top of the piano waiting to hear her purr and twitch music."

"I love you, honey," Judd said. "This economic downturn won't last forever. "Let's think of something to cheer us during these two weeks."

Molly, in a happy voice, almost sang, "Oh ho, my dear, I already have."

"Well, tell me about it." Judd's laughter was contagious.

"I'm going to host a concert," Molly assured her puzzled husband. And, Honey, you'll be here for it. I've already checked the dates. It'll be entirely choral music! Music such as you've never heard."

"Now wait a minute . . . . You're teasing me. Have you booked the Mormon Tabernacle Choir?"

"No, of course not. My choral group will be singing *a cappella.*"

"O.K. I give up. May I wake the kids? I can't wait to see our babies. And get your thoughts together. You've had too much tea, Mama Love. Like I said, 'this downturn' . . . ."

". . . . won't last forever." Molly finished his sentence. "See you at the concert, Daddy. It's set for Friday night, August 8. Now go wake your babies, but be sure you get them back to sleep."

The next day, Sunday, Judd was tired from his intense preparation for Pentagon training and opted to stay at home and prepare lunch for his family while all was quiet. Molly, of course, was church organist and carefully serenaded the congregants with those rich velvety chords escaping the pipes. The youngsters enjoyed children's church in another part of the building, and there were the McCrary boys wearing new blue suits, "and the girls dressed up even morether," reported Tark later at lunch.

After church, Molly ran into prospective new neighbors, Catherine and Vann Collins, who announced their plans to move to Piney Paths on August 2. ("Just in time for the concert," Molly whispered gleefully to herself.) Catherine was an architect and building contractor all in one, and Vann was her business manager.

Like her soon-to-be neighbor, she also answered to a descriptive name: "Catherine-the-Great," awarded by her progeny, Jenny, Stacy, and Lee. Prior to the naming, however, the children obtained approval from "Honestly," their in-house grandmother and Catherine's mother-in-law.

Catherine had no training in architecture other than by osmosis from sitting at her father's drafting table while he designed structures of his day under the illusion that, young as he was, he'd be the next Frank Lloyd Wright.

Searching for the lot on which to place the family's new home, she quickly found it, knowing immediately that 4609 would be the number of the house, though her husband and sons advised her friend against the location (too far out). In consultation with "Honestly," however, she was convinced that it was for them. Daughter Jenny agreed, as well.

Now, Catherine thought, how do we get the males on board? It didn't take long. They adjusted immediately when they found a branch running through their property and the other two big yards on their side of the street. "What a find!" exclaimed the boys; "What a find!" Racing down-hill to jump into the water, they were ecstatic. Puffing and blowing back up hill, however, was not easy—especially with the deterrent of long wet britches and high top rubber-soled shoes. (What did their dad—a former New Yorker—mean when he called boys "Knickerbockers?") Catherine, who told her sons to "look it up," suddenly became "Not-so-Great."

"We're watching for the moving truck—or wagon?—on August 2," called Molly. "Be sure to put Friday night, the 8th, on your calendar . . . . What? . . . . No, honey, your whole family. 'Honestly'? Of course Vann's mother's invited. Singers *a cappella!* You'll get an invitation, including Honestly. No, no! In my back yard under those lovely trees."

Before Molly could get out of her Sunday clothes, a telephone call she didn't want to hear was waiting. On the line, her friend Phyllis, sounded distraught, as through her tears, she said, "Molly, I know I haven't given you time to have lunch, but if you could come over for just a few minutes before the afternoon ends, I would be so grateful. You're so ready to listen, and I—to put it plainly—need your calm presence. If you even consider this request, why not wait 'til about four? That would give you time to rest a little after your all-day Saturday lessons."

Molly answered, "Dear, dear Phyllis, forget the Saturday marathon. I'll come now. Or at four. Or, for that matter, at midnight. Whenever suits you best, Little Phil."

"About four, please, Molly. I'll get myself together before then."

"Four it is then, dear. I'll be there."

"Thanks so much. I'll look forward to your company. Bye, bye, Mama Molly." Phyllis hung up the phone.

Judd was putting lunch on the table, the kids were already seated, and Molly decided to wear her Sunday best and be careful not to spill gravy on her blouse.

"Who was on the phone, Molly Love?" It was typical of Judd to ask.

"Little Phil next door. She wanted me to come over at four to talk some business. She was afraid I was tired from all the piano lessons yesterday."

Judd saw no need for comment, so he turned to the kids to ask who'd say Grace.

"Oh. let me, Daddy," pleaded Terry, a five-year-old unabashed whiz.

In broken phrases, he prayed, "Dear God, thank you for Mama Molly and my Major daddy and his army. And thank you for the lunch he made by hisself. Bless all my sisters and my little brother. A-men."

"I'm **not** your little brother, I was borned first. My daddy said so. Don't say that, Terry, no morether," Tark spoke adamantly.

"I want to see you two on the back porch for a minute, boys. Please excuse yourselves."

Strangely, not another voice was heard at the table until Judd and the twins returned. After a self-imposed quiet time, Terry could wait no longer to tell a story: "In Sunday school," he said, "my teacher was askin' George to sit down, but George didn't sit down. No sir, he didn't sit down at all. In a minute, she said, 'George, when I ask you to do something, I would 'preciate it if you'd act like you heard me. You're not deaf, by any chance, are you?' Old George sat down quick, but it was in Mary Lou's chair, and Mary Lou was in it, but she stood up just in time 'cause . . . and the teacher said, "George, I know you saw Mary Lou in her chair before you sat down."

George said immediately, "I did. I saw her, but if my mama'd been here, she'd've said, 'Ther morether merrier."

"What did your teacher say then?" asked Trish through her snickers.

"Oh, she didn't say any more. She just laughed out loud like the other teacher did."

What a lovely Sunday lunch the McCrary bunch shared. But when the girls cleared the table and Marianne washed dishes, it was time for Molly finally to change clothes and get comfortable for her visit next door. She had tried to second guess the obvious difficulty in Little Phil's life, but she had no idea, no clue, and no understanding of her or of what Big Phil's dilemma might be—or if a dilemma was involved—at all. She rang the doorbell.

Phyllis might have lost hope in something or someone earlier; however, Molly's first glimpse of her at the door erased the fear for her friend. Instead, she thought of Wordsworth's beautiful "My heart leaps up when I behold a rainbow in the sky . . . ."

"Phyllis, you're like a rainbow . . . or maybe 'a row of golden daffodils' . . . What happened between noon and now?"

Phyllis took Molly to the living room and, before they even moved toward the new chairs, thanked her for coming on a day of rest. Then the explanation began: "You probably thought I was upset when I called you and maybe you decided it was because Phil wasn't here. And you were right. Neither he nor his car could be seen. But let me quickly say that he left not because there's something wrong with our marriage. It was just that something's wrong with our world. Molly, Phil went to Raleigh to enlist and then try to get a commission."

"Bless your heart, Phyllis. I admit I'm surprised because of Phil's law practice. I thought he'd be safe for decades." said Molly.

"Well, Phil's law practice hasn't been booming . . . ."

Even so, dear, they say this is a short downturn. Was that the reason for his enlisting?" asked Molly.

"Mama Molly, I suppose you know Phil as well as anyone. He didn't want to serve in the military; but, oh, how he wanted to serve in the military."

"I'm a little confused, I guess," confessed Molly.

"This is what I can tell you about Phil's own confusion. (He's had that malady, too, dear.)"

"As have you, Phyllis." Molly mustered a very slight smile. "My dear husband does not want to leave us. He adores his children, you know. And he loves me, too, I might add."

"And his country, as well. I think you're headed there," contributed Molly.

"Right, mind reader. But that still wasn't at the heart of his decision. Phil's faith was strongly involved in this, and you know how he's always been about living right." Phyllis sighed. "Continuing, Molly, he would give his life before he'd hide from having to fight for this country . . . . He'd never sneak off to, to . . . anywhere else, to avoid the draft. That's where we are right now." Phyllis's tears returned, and Molly's joined hers.

"It's like this: the nation of his birth has become the nation of his heart," offered Molly. "And that's not all: This decision was something like an act of saving grace for your Big Philip."

Family? Yes, family. Molly could have gotten lost in the story of Phil's decision; however, it came back to her to ask about the return of Philip to his home next door. "He'll be back by the 8th of August, won't he? I'm hosting a choral concert in my back yard the night of the 8th. ALL your family must come. It's a wonderful chorale. Even the children will be mesmerized.

"Count on it, Molly. I can hardly wait," Phyllis said as they embraced in mutual understanding. "And thanks."

Until Phyllis and Philip became neighbors to Molly and Judd, they answered to normal names as they had always. Then the young name changers on Piney Paths got busy. After "Mama Molly" and "Catherine the Great," "Little Phyl" and "Big Phil" became more familiar on the street. The former was the name for Phyllis, the mother, and the latter for Philip, the dad. In the meantime, they were so proud that their four boys (two sets of twins), wanted their parents to have fun names, too. So Edwin and Allen, 7, and Cameron and Clay, 5, did the naming. Big Phil said to all in earshot, "Now weren't those boys clever, though, to give those nicknames to their mom and dad?"

Phyllis taught third grade arithmetic in Sandy Hills Elementary School, while Philip was an attorney on Main Street. He was also a hero of sorts because he had been a football star at his high school in Virginia. "Welcome to the Conrads—Phyllis, Phil, Edwin, Allen, Clay, and Cameron."

Mother Molly announced the arrival of all her concert goers as they came into her yard at 7:45, on August 8, 1941, eager to hear the beautiful music of a most unusual choral group. It would start at 8:00.

Once all concert goers settled in their "opera chairs," Mama Molly took a microphone to a small lectern in the center front of a large back yard. About fifty comfortable chairs were set up in the middle, facing the lectern, while on either side of the chairs were dozens of' trees of several species, with pines and oaks being predominant. Outdoor lanterns provided bright lighting for the guests to chat in the event the musicians might be a bit later than expected.

Mama Molly walked assuredly to the podium. "Is she going to direct?" asked a man near the front.

"No one heard an answer," the hostess said in her voice of musical expectations.

One more word, please. You will likely not see any of the musicians tonight—at least not face to face. But feel free to give them ovations as you wish.

There is a director. Her choir is in two very large sections of this yard. It is quite amazing that she has them so well disciplined. Thank you. Applause, please." *(Commanding applause, lights out, tiny noises in the trees.)*

August 8, 1941 Dear Mrs. McCrary,

> *Thank you more than I can say for inviting me to the magnificent concert in your beautiful surroundings. How can I express my enjoyment? I will try:*
>
> *Softly, crickets, cicadas, grasshoppers, katydids, all, serenaded us from the oaks to our right. A complete stop followed.*
>
> *Within seconds, a crescendo from pines and oaks, both sides, began in perfect pitch, precise timing, growing in volume 'til no other sound surpassed it. Then, it slowed, as directed, until a livelier score gave us an irresistibly sweet melodic chorus.*

In perfect precision, minor chords, left, chilled us as the director signaled, right, for soft and lovely. I didn't know who or what handled the baton as this choral cacophany blessed me and the summer evening with as beautiful a concert as one's emotions could bear to hear for a little night music.

I thanked God for the crickets. But I wasn't sure to which singers should go a curtsy.

*They sang softly at times before bringing the house down with a **Hallelujah Chorus** of their own understanding. The audience stood. Some wept. All cheered, applauded.*

Now I can think of it, picture it, hear it, and brush a tear from my cheek.

Very gratefully yours,
Honestly Collins

Honestly's response was one of several that expressed similar reactions. Mama Molly was elated until she had to think of Judd's having to head for the Pentagon in less than a week. She said out loud, "Lord God, Please take care of him, wherever he has to go. Amen."

Wherever Judd had to go, he broke the news by phone when he called her to say he had good news on two fronts: "Molly Love, I've made Lieutenant Colonel! Got my silver leaf today! The other thing I have to tell you is that I won't be coming back to Bragg for a bit, Molly. My heart hurts that I won't see you before I go."

"Go WHERE? Judd!"
He laughed. "They're sending me to Hawaii. How about that? From the heat of Fort Bragg, in the summer, to the paradise of the Islands. I can't believe it."
Neither could Molly. But new colonels had to travel . . . .

1942

Glory's Gift Goes to Neighborhood Library

Like public schools, Black communities in Sandy Hills, North Carolina, were segregated during the years of World Wars I and II, the Great Depression, and other societal problems of the early-to-mid 20th Century and even later into the '50s.

A family of black neighbors became friends of Lily and Lil soon after they moved into the upstairs apartment, which, as Lil said, "suits Mom and me to a T." The neighbors, who lived nearby on a winding street, a half mile away, were Marvin and O'Zella Steele, their daughter, Glory, 15, and their son, Marcus, 17. Laura, Lily's best friend, introduced the Steeles, who had come to pick up her laundry on a Saturday morning." In the introduction, Lily became "Mrs. McNeill," but Laura used first names only in introducing the black couple.

Lil squirmed and politely asked their last name. "Oh, now, we're O'Zella and Marvin, and we're fine with whichever names you use." Marvin said.

First on one foot and then the other, he removed his hat and said to Lily, "Didn't Miss Laura say you're Miss McNeill?"

Lily replied, "That she did, but I'm Mrs. McNeill. Do you know some other folks with our name?"

"Yes'm. There's lots of 'em. The best man I ever knew was one of a kind, though. I'm speakin' of Mr. Neal McNeill. See, I was once the butcher in his store down on the square. You know, not many stores downtown would have a colored man for any job, but 'specially as a butcher, seems to me. Mr. Neal was a prince of a man. I sure loved 'im."

Lily took Marvin's hand. "Well, of course. I heard him speak of you hundreds of times, Marvin. He loved you, too." Marvin quickly turned his head the other way.

Laura couldn't believe this coincidence. But she couldn't remain unmoved. She loved Neal, too, but all she could do was put her arm around Lily; O'Zella took the cue and did the same. "What a lovely occasion this has been," said Laura.

O'Zella asked, "Is it all right to call you Miss Lily?"

Lily replied, "I'll call you O'Zella if you'll call me Lily."

O'Zella whooped with laughter. "Let's do it," she exclaimed. But she had one more thing to say: "You won't believe it, Mrs. McN. . . . Miss Lily . . . Lily . . . .

That was Marvin's time to break into the conversation, also *with one more thing to say:* "You're not believin' this, but O'Zella and me live on *McNeill Street!*"

Still laughing at the coincidence, all but Lil, who had a baby-sitting job, moved to the green lawn chairs to talk further. Marvin said, "Mrs. McNeill, will it be all right if O'Zella and me call on you this afternoon? We'd like to tell you about our laundry business."

O'Zella sat up straighter in her chair.

Lily said, "So you've started your own laundry business. I like your vitality in hard times."

"Yes, ma'am. It's what we do, and it's a pretty good business, thank the Lord," declared Marvin.

"Of course you may talk to me about your work. Please do come," invited Lily. Continuing, she gave them directions. "The house across the street is where my daughter and I live now. Our apartment's upstairs on the right. Oops! Let me run home and straighten up a little. I didn't know we were going to have company. Should I get some of our wash together for you to take?" Lily envisioned the hamper of laundry already full and needing attention.

O'Zella had her turn: "You hear that, Marvin? Mrs. McNeill—uh, Lily—is nice enough to have us come without talkin' her ears off about washin' and ironin'"

"That'll be nice, Miss Lily. We do towels, bed clothes, regular clothes for men and women, and children's stuff, too. If the customer provides the wash, we provide a washpot full of hot sudsy water every day. O'Zella does the main finishing, and some friends in the neighborhood then help her with ironin' and stuff. Now my wife is the best in the world with havin' things look nice." Marvin grinned at his wife and leaned back in his chair.

"Well. I've hit the jackpot today," said Lily. What's your schedule?

"We pick up on Saturday, and your clothes will be back to you on Wednesday. And, oh yes, Miss Lily, the first time is free. Since we've already signed up, so to speak, we'll just follow you to your place, pick up your stuff, and go get started. All right?" Marvin stood to leave.

"More than all right," Lily agreed. The Steeles loaded their truck and set out for McNeill Street.

"Late on Wednesday afternoon, Lil read by an open window in the living room. She stopped to be sure she heard what she needed to be sure of. There. It came again, louder this time: "Leel! Here your clothes, Leel. I'm Glory. I got your clothes!" Lil dashed downstairs to find Glory, if indeed, it was she at all. It had to be: the laundry the small young girl carried was quite recognizable as belonging to Lil and Lily.

"Oh, thanks, Glory, I'm Lil. Could you possibly help me carry some of this sweet-smelling stuff upstairs?" Glory agreed. "Listen, Glory, it's wonderful of you to deliver it so promptly. Can you come in for a Co-Cola?" She did, indeed, want to come in.

"It's a litle scary when you deliver laundry to somebody you've never seen before," Glory confessed.

Lil laid the two bundles on her own bed and led her guest through the kitchen—Cokes for each—into the living room, which a visitor might guess to be a library. This visitor was impressed with the sheer number of volumes—even "no comic books for Marcus, and no movie magazines for me," she pondered.

"Do you like to read?" Lil asked.

"Oh, yes'm," Glory answered. "I do a lot of reading in the library at my school."

"What's your favorite book?" Lil wondered.

Glory giggled, her hand over her mouth. "I'm not real sure of my very, very favorite, but I really, really like *Jane Eyre*, by Charlotte Bronte. What do you like to read?"

Lil was surprised. "Here you are, Glory Steele—two years younger than I, and you're already into the Bronte novels?"

"Well, I started that one in my school library and didn't get to finish before another student needed it. But I also like Little Women. Jo's my favorite."

"So do I," agreed Lil. "And Jo's my favorite, too."

Glory stood to go. "Thank you for the soda," she said. "It was good."

"Can you hang on for a second, Glory? I want to show you something." Lil walked over to one of the book shelves, removed a volume, wrote something in it, and handed it to her new friend. "I want you to have this," she said warmly.

Glory gasped and reached eagerly for the book. She said, in a trembly voice, "Oh, it's Jane Eyre! The first book in my very own library! Thank you, Lil. Thank you."

"You're so welcome. Don't forget to look inside the front cover. I wrote something there I want you to read."

Glory couldn't wait to turn to that cover page: "To Glory, my book reading friend. All the best, Lil."

She embraced her new (but historic) book and was excited to have a friend named Lil, who also liked to read. Glory hopped and skipped through the pathways all the way back to McNeill Street. "Jane Eyre," she whispered with each happy step. "The first book in my own personal library!" Glory restated the truth. And she'd say it twice more before reaching home.

Some toil in modest neighborhoods, where sandy yards swept smooth
upstage the gray wood siding and front shutters painted green.
Some Lilies polish hardwood floors in dream homes of their years,
where fenced-in lawns and stepping stones lead to a gold fish pool
beneath the weeping willows.

1943

Sandy Hills, North Carolina and Camp Snyderman, USA

The small-but-not-too-small town grew among the pine trees and white sandy dunes of the beautiful state of North Carolina. The old 'Possum Creek flowed not too far down an old rural highway out of town, and Sandy Hills boasted of having the creek's namesake, O'Possum Pond. It was good for fishing and for recreation and celebrations nearby. A selfless builder or two had constructed an attractive club house on the lake (pond) for reserved club meetings, parties, and dancing.

That's not all: Sandy Hills was also the county seat of its county, which was a proud identity for the town that bustled with commercial activity all week, especially on Saturday. In the 1930s and later, Sunday was the big day for Baptists, Methodists, Presbyterians, Episcopalians, and smaller denominations. It was a happy town that well knew how to be sad during trying times but was always grateful for the common life of good neighbors, fertile farmland, well-run cotton mills within shouting distance, and every sort of business imaginable. Sandy Hills residents facetiously identified old timers and newcomers alike by their walk, their accent, their laughter, and by how many brothers, sisters, and in-laws lived in the same house. And by "who's your daddy?" Without hesitation, strangers usually joined the jocularity. It's true: everybody knew everybody else. Lil once asked Neal, her father, why so many people in town had the same last name as theirs. Neal laughed and said, "Honey, in Sandy Hills, there are hoe handle McNeills and kid glove McNeills. Altogether, we're a crowd."

Lil was left to her imagination. She pondered, but she made herself believe in her heart that he was somewhere in the middle.

He was quite ambitious and well respected, but she had never seen him wear kid gloves. Yet, she had watched him many times with hoe in hand—out by the melons growing on his farm, or the cucumbers in his back yard at home.

The town was hardly a backward place; it was, indeed, a small city destined never to claim BIG city status—at least not in the 20th Century—if ever. Apparently it still holds to that identity, but then, in the 1940s, Sandy Hills introduced itself to thousands of new people from Chicago, Boston, New York City, Los Angeles, and Key West, among the throngs from other recognizable home towns: maybe Omaha or Atlanta even. Or Cincinnati.

Camp Snyderman had come to town. Not literally but more than figuratively. It was a new air base the United States planted soon after the declaration of World War II, strictly for air-borne special forces, such as glider pilots and paratroopers (Lily's observation). They didn't know what they had until the convoys started rolling through Main Street, and the sidewalk traffic downtown displayed more boots than loafers and saddle shoes, the latter noticeably scruffy compared to the highly polished military foot wear.

One Saturday morning, Lily decided to go to the office a little early because of her load of work left from Friday, afraid, as she was that otherwise she would have to miss out on her half day off. Her policy was to do no housework on Saturday afternoon if at all possible. Was this a new day? Did Lily not work at home every minute she was there? Lil was a bit jealous because she had already lined up two baby-sitting jobs in the neighborhood: little two-year-old Harry from across the street, 1:00-3:00 o'clock, and five-year-old "Miss Memory," whose military parents had rented a cottage in the side-yard garden at Laura's. Lil would take care of the little girl at 7:00 for her parents to see an early movie.

"See you about lunch time, Hon," Lily called to Lil. When she didn't come in by noon, Lil put her mom's salad into the refrigerator (at last they had one that worked) to keep fresh. She would go on over to her baby sitting job and see Mom afterwards.

Harry's folks came in exactly at 3:00, whirled him in the air, and thanked Lil profusely as they handed her the going rate of 25 cents an hour. Lil loved earning money and jiggled the pair of quarters in her jacket pocket as she walked home.

"What a pretty spring day," she noticed, thinking, "Wonder if Mom's home yet?" Even as she questioned, she approached Laura's pretty side yard with the wooden lawn chairs freshly painted green. "Hey, Mom," she called as she spotted Lily, Laura, and Katy relaxing in the chairs and decided to join them. She was greeted warmly by the women, and Lily was relieved that Lil was poised enough to return their gracious welcome. After the polite acknowledgments, Lil turned to Lily: "Mom, I was worried that you were late coming home for lunch today. You must've had more to do than . . . ."

Lily interrupted, "No, it wasn't that. I simply had to wait at the Presbyterian Church corner for a half hour before I could cross the street."

"What in the world?" Lil started. The other women answered, having already heard the story, all talking at once, eyes big, excited about the news of what's going on with the military complex in "our back yard." But they heard the news again as Lily repeated the long wait at the corner.

"It was a convoy," Lily said, sighing. "And it was long. All these army vehicles creeping through town at about two miles an hour and just packed with soldiers . . . . I felt so sorry for those boys; they looked so tired. You be cautious, Lil, honey?"

Lil laughed and promised as her mother had directed. Laura squirmed in her green chair and said, "That reminds me, Lily. You know my girls are old enough to be friendly with these soldiers. In fact, they should have been home an hour ago . . . ."

Facing the street, Lil craned her neck enough to recognize Kate and Melinda, Laura's daughters. "I think I see them now, Miss Laura. They have some soldiers with them but they seem to be enjoying the company."

"My land, Lil, what are we going to do with all this?" Miss Laura was enjoying her girls' attraction to young men—or *vice versa.*

Lil answered with a giggle.

At the precise moment of a sense of unease, Kate and Melinda turned into the yard — as did the four airmen who were keeping them company.

Kate said, "Mama, we didn't invite them to come."

Melinda, the older daughter, added, "They're just as nice as they can be, Mama."

The boys laughed and introduced themselves. So Earl, Rick, Jim, and Hal plunked down on the grass, even though the mannerly women offered their chairs. The conversation was delightful, the young men seemed to love the company, and could they come again sometime soon? Please? They did that. Frequently. Earl, the youngest of the boys, even asked Lily if he could visit her daughter sometime. He did, and soon became a regular Sunday evening dinner guest. But Lil was so young. "Aw, Mom," she'd say.

But would Mom ever get out of the kitchen?

At least two of those four airmen dated some of the Sandy Hills teens, and older girls, too, including Melinda. Rick even later married a local young woman, who happily moved with him to Pennsylvania, his long-time home.

Lil still was young for serious romance; however, she enjoyed the teenage version anyway. When only a tenth-grader, her serious crush was on a high school senior, and "the minute he received his high school diploma," Lil said, "he was drafted and shipped to the Pacific."

"Such is life in war time," Lily reminded her daughter but was a bit concerned that "the serious crush" wrote Lil a letter every day, to which the teen responded. Every day.

Lily's own brother had been captured in the Philippines and remained a prisoner of war of the Japanese army for four years. "But he came home after that," Lil offered. The family had always called him "Bubber," and Lil, at every mention of that name, reminded all within earshot that her own dad was "Big Bubber," so named by the same proud relatives.

Once Sandy Hills relaxed a bit regarding the long convoys and the planes flying over and the young men in uniform seeking female companionship, they began to notice with great interest the contributions that some of the airmen were adding to lifestyles of the locals; for example, retail sales were improving in many of the stores, and that alone helped the economy. An eating place or two appeared on the streets downtown, giving the long-standing familiar cafe some space at lunch time, and encouraging one of the barbecue places to remodel and add tables along with the colorful new look of an experienced interior decorator. A classy motel even appeared on the highway into town. As frightening as war news was, it kept the town up-to-date on information—good or bad. Interestingly, some unpleasant everyday details seemed farther away than before.

Two noteworthy incidents occurred in Lily and Lil's lives. For example, the choir at their church gained a marvelous baritone voice, courtesy of an actor/singer who brought his talent to church on some Sundays before accepting the invitation to sing every weekend. People of the war years would recognize his name and home town, but suffice it to say, so did the organist/choir director, "What a difference a trained voice makes." She complimented the local sopranos and tenors. By this time Lil had begun using her young voice in the soprano section "but would wait to perform my first solo," she joked.

The second incident was Lily's delight to tell—if only because it was hers and hers only: When two men in uniform came into the office on a quiet afternoon to transact some business, only she was available to answer their needs. One soldier, in particular, was pleasant in relating his wishes to Lily, who could handle them with no problems. And did. As the men turned to leave, the tall, handsome one turned to thank her again. His friend, the quiet one, said to Lily, "Ma'am, I must tell you something that you may not have realized: you have just been helpful to the famous Western star, Marshall Mason!"

Was Lily doubtful or believing? "No! You're teasing me." The star grinned as he reached for her hand. His friend beamed. And Lily graciously returned the hand gesture while they stood smiling for a quiet moment before the star bowed grandly and left. Lily graciously reacted after the fact that this famous personality had been a part of her daily routine. Now the only way she could have used the moment was from Jim's wife, Libby, who knew all about the cowboy shows on the radio and in the movies. (Lily had no radio at this stage of her life, and rarely did she spend a quarter to see a movie.) But Angie assured her that pleasure would be Lily's response to the *N.C. Today* story her sister-in-law would be writing for the paper. On hearing the news, Libby, who was adept at repeating local happenings, informed Lily that the famous actor must have been, in real life, Lew Hazelton, who apparently was alive and well in his role at the time. He hadn't signed his name in the business transaction, so Libby had no clue as to his real life identity. But it must be Hazelton, she insisted. Lily wasn't inspired further to trace the actor's name; she was simply pleased that his fame, had somehow touched her usually uneventful life.

By the end of that week, Lily and Lil checked out the radios at Hills' Furniture Store and wasted no time buying one. What a treasure it came to be. The two chronic tuners-in at last learned easily to laugh. Not that there was a lack of laughter all through life, hard as events of the times presented themselves. But nights after chores were done, the three-member McNeill family had loved sitting together by the warmth of the fire and sharing childhood memories. More recently, in the larger clan, particularly on Lily's side of the family, her witty siblings— and their spouses—could keep even "toilers" and "spinners" extremely amused—especially when Lily and her two younger sisters created bearable puns. Also, when they were together— they were teased unmercifully as "The Sisters of the Patriotic hair"; i.e., Lily's hair was auburn with red highlights; Tina's, (the youngest—30 something) was prematurely platinum white, and Sis's was gray and tinted with a blue rinse.

But radio shows such as *Fibber McGee and Molly, Jack Benny,* and *Red Skelton* were real American colors for side-splitting laughter.

1944

The Editor's Editorial

The then recently named editor of a large newspaper in another Southern state was in a situation indeed when his lead editorial in the Saturday *News and Views*—just then hitting the streets—seriously chastised the high sheriff of a certain county seat for selling moonshine from his personal still, halfway up a mountain, near his country home.

Many of the townspeople were incensed that the editor—he not even an elected official—could so demean the sheriff by criticizing him in the local press. The lead into the article's second editorial paragraph started as follows:

Of all law enforcement personnel, the Sheriff should certainly know what is legal and what is not—THAT IS, IF HE'S SERVING HIS CONSTITUENTS AS HE IS SWORN TO DO. He has maliciously broken the law and must face the consequences.

The sheriff's supporters seethed but found some comfort in the news that a group of outspoken legislators over in the state capitol were threatening to pass a law supporting said sheriff. "It will never happen. Not in this state," growled a pro-sheriff grouch.

"This kind of smut can't be tolerated," bellowed Sgt. Melvin, making derogatory remarks about so-called "freedom of the press."

In the meantime down at the newspaper office, a few well-meaning backers of the editorial were in hot pursuit of justice. "The fact that all law abiding citizens should have engraved on their brains is the very one declaring stills and moonshine illegal," they barked.

Editor Linderman walked out of his office about four o'clock, the time he customarily drank a cup of coffee. Was he aware, the office visitors wondered, that he was under fire? Know it or not, he was cheered and applauded, slapped on the back, raucously congratulated for his bravery in stating the illegality of the sheriff's money-making scheme. Did he know he was in trouble? They couldn't tell. He simply took his coffee, and a cup for his assistant, who was with him in a rather confidential conference at the time.

In a half-hour, a self-appointed posse appeared with handcuffs, demanding to see the editor. Not waiting for an answer, they simply flung open his office door and burst through. Fortunately, the editorial two were still sipping coffee in their business meeting at this crucial time of discontent surrounding the press and its freedom . . . or not.

Editor Linderman stood immediately. He questioned the men. "Sirs, what can I do for you?" Officer Melvin slapped the handcuffs on the news man, who was surprised at first but had suddenly caught on. About four seconds had passed.

"So you didn't like my editorial, huh? On what charges are you arresting me?"

It was Melvin again, rushing to answer first: "A newspaper man's got no right to do what you done—wrote—about the high sheriff."

"Have you not heard—even yet—of freedom of the press? Or the illegal act Sheriff Whittier's been committing? Listen, if you're really going to lock me up, I've got to call my wife. I've got to," he pleaded.

Forget it. Nobody's calling your wife. Certainly not you!

Annabelle Teague, the assistant editor, sent Ben Linderman a signal that Ben understood. He relaxed and smiled slightly as he passed his group of supporters. He felt strangely calm as he walked by Annabelle. She'd notify Mary; he knew she would.

The phone rang at Mary and Ben Linderman's home at precisely 5:30 p.m. "Mary, this is Annabelle," were the words that were fraught with concern reaching Mary Linderman's ear. But in five minutes, the whole report from 'Belle stirred Mary to action. She and 'Belle talked on for, say, another ten minutes while they discussed their own roles in the stressful situation.

The phone rang at the Presbyterian manse about 5:50. Dr. Baldwin-Smith answered, discovering Mary Linderman at the other end of the line wanting desperately to speak to the minister's wife, Elizabeth. All he heard was his wife's promise to Mary: "Bless you, Mary. I'll meet you at the jail at 7:00. No, I think Brad shouldn't join us. Let's show our feminine principles and strength."

The phone rang at Madge Penegar's house at 6:07. Her teen-aged son, Mike, answered the phone with "Hello. This is the home of Congressman Penegar's family. My father is at the State Capitol, May I . . . . ? Oh, you want my mother. Just a moment, please . . . ."

" . . . . Mary, dear, hello! I'm distressed to hear, just ten minutes ago, about Ben. What can I do?" After five minutes the call was over. Madge ended the conversation when she agreed to meet Mary, Annabelle, and Elizabeth at 7:00.

At 6:35, Ben Linderman was miserably asking himself why this was happening. Then he asked God. "Did I make a terrible mistake, Lord? If I did, please forgive me, and reveal to me Your will. I thought I had sensed Your approval before I ever wrote the piece. I really did. Please help me!"

His next plea for help was to Mary, "How in the world did I ever land here, for crying out loud? Mary, darling, rescue me!" he called out in a loud voice, but it became weaker as the warden entered to report that several cars had just parked outside. Ben continued pleading with his wife, "Mary, hurry! They're coming to lynch me! I can't go through this without you. MARY?"

Ben surprised himself that he could say, "Oh, God, I suddenly feel at peace. I know I did not commit a sin. Thank You for hearing my prayer."

Just as he sat on the edge of his bumpy cot, ending his prayer of gratitude, she walked in. "Darling, is it really you?" He almost cried—until she embraced him and whispered, "You have company, dearest."

When he looked beyond her, his cell door creaked open, and there stood Annabelle, Elizabeth Baldwin-Smith, Madge Penegar, and his dear Mary. He couldn't make his voice work well enough to thank them profusely for being there. "What next?" was an assuring word from each of the women. He felt better. So much better.

He was thinking later, he told Mary, that four women on a mission can accomplish great things. "God be with you," he called out to them. He knew the powerful persuasiveness of this group, anyway.

The mystery began. 'Belle called for Judge Richardson to issue an order for every police officer in the building to meet in one of the small courtrooms upstairs. Pronto!

The 14 men in uniform, led by Officer Merton, scrambled up the steps (no elevators after 7:30 p.m.) and rushed for chairs. "But where was that weasel—that judge . . . Judge Richardson, was it?" Suddenly they decided, "Judge Richardson had been replaced by . . . these four WOMEN!" If the scene about to begin were introducing a contemporary stage production, the printed program would have informed the audience as follows: (Please turn the page.)

Enter:

Four outstanding women of the community, who take their seats at a large table in the center front courtroom.

Annabelle Teague, assistant editor for the *News and Views*, *presiding*

Elizabeth Baldwin-Smith, *representing* "Citizens for Morality" Madge Penegar, *President*, "Women for Justice" Mary Linderman, *Vice President*, Woman's Club

Conference in Session

Annabelle Teague (pounding a gavel)

"The meeting will come to order, please. Thank you for responding to Judge Richardson's mandate to attend . . . ."

❧ ❧ ❧ ❧ ❧ ❧

The headlines of the Saturday *News and Views* by **Annabelle Teague, assistant editor, read, "Peace in the Hills, Peace in the Valleys." The lead story began**

Within a half hour after midnight Friday, Judge Paul Richardson, 14 local police officers, and Acting County Sheriff James J. Whittier witnessed destruction of an illicit distillery formerly owned and operated by Whittier. The property and the related sales of moonshine whiskey therefrom were declared illegal upon recent discovery by state inspectors.

Plans, Celebrations

V. J. Day in 1945

"Planning should definitely get under way," said the Mayor:

Around the world news reports of the atom bombs falling on Hiroshima and Nagasaki, Japan, seemed to hint that such massive destruction by our own forces would cause cessation in a short time of the almost four-year long battle between Japan and the United States. The bombing occurred in Hiroshima on August 6, 1945, and in Nagasaki on the 7th. VJ Day was officially celebrated on August 14, although "the official surrender accords would not be signed until September 2." (*The Dispatch,* August 13, 1945)

The months stretched into hopelessness 'til troops came home again.
Music playing! Streets for dancing! Embracing, Laughter, Joy!
But prayers of hope came from those hearts, both broken and relieved,
as loved ones knew for sure the costs they'd paid or lost in war.
They'd trust Him for the future.

Planning ahead was one of the mayor's priorities:

At a meeting three days before the scheduled V.J. Day celebration in Sandy Hills, a positive note was contagious in the gathering room at the local fire station.

"Suggestions wanted!" A legitimate plea came from the town manager, who occupied the presiding officer's chair.

"I have one, Billy," offered a committee member. "I was thinking who could get the folks all revved up for a celebration at the right time. Is there a lady musician who could do that?"

"If we could get some of the women who were on blackout duty all those nights, it would add authenticity," stated the male president of one of the nearby colleges.

"Good thought, Doctor, who would . . . . ?

"Mrs. McCrary!" shouted a councilman who needed to be heard. "There's no better musician or finer person in all of Sandy Hills. And can she organize a group? You bet." The nine-member committee elected the nominee without question and immediately appointed (by acclamation) the mayor to invite her.

"Mama Molly" accepted the challenge and so told the mayor as she welcomed his invitation. "Since my husband, Judd, was shipped to the Pacific, I've been volunteering for blackout duty for a couple of months myself. Thank you, Mr. Mayor."

"No. Thank *you*, Mrs. McCrary."

It was all carefully planned:

When the fire bell clanged without sounding a specific number at the main station in Sandy Hills, one knew something extraordinary was happening. But where? What? Had the time come?

In the early afternoon the downtown churches rang bells and played organ music set on "loud." Some accordion music was also reported, or so the rumors hinted. Capt. Roberts, the fire chief, ordered two drivers of a hook and ladder giant to crank engines and sound sirens as early as 6:00 p.m., while the chief took command from a small rear platform on the town's red monster. "By the time the fire wagons reached the designated spot, half the population of the town had turned out," so guessed Capt. Roberts.

The police stopped traffic all the way from the square down to the Presbyterian Church corner. At the sounds of drum rolls and trumpets, the Sandy Hills High School band marched from the starting point to the designated spot. At a brief siren signal from Capt. Roberts' rear platform, all the lights in town shone forth in obedience to the mayor's edict that house lights, street lights, flash lights, office and warehouse lights, and headlights of moving vehicles participate.

At the appointed time, a line of women in blackout garb offered an impressive imitation of the Rockettes in the center of Main Street as the band played Vera Lynn's great song, "When the Lights Go On Again All Over the World." By then, the street was packed with lines of onlookers, some creating their own dance steps, some cheering noisily, and a few even teary-eyed. Mrs McCrary and the dancers were hailed loudly and proudly; however, in lieu of the requested encores, they curtsied time and again to the appreciative audience. It was a night to behold.

When Mother Molly, exuberant as she already was after hearing just two days ago that her husband, Lt. Col. Judson McCrary, was recovering nicely from a broken foot, after having jumped away from an exploding land mine, and would return home in a week or so. With their mother, all six of the McCrary children were beaming with pride at the news of their dad and at the star power of their mother and her dancers.

Her now six-year-old twin boys were prepared when she asked what they enjoyed most about the night's celebration. Tark hastened to answer, "If I'd seen that sailor kissing a girl, I'd've liked it morether."

Terry explained, "You remember, Mama, the picture in the newspaper at the drug store this afternoon: the one from New York, you said." (*Laughter and rowdy applause from the crowd were almost deafening.*)

Lilies During and After Wartime

The Lilies aged in World War II, so young in World War I,
hid tears and fears from their young tots when Moms, too, wished to hide.
They shed their tears at fright'ning news of brothers, husbands, sons:
"Missing!" screamed the telegrams, but where from and for how long?
Tell us! Say it isn't so!

Lilies toiled in northern war plants, built planes and ships and guns
while back home Granny took the kids to school and Sunday school,
made gravy faces in their grits and boiled their eggs just right.
She assured them gently that their parents miss them, too.
*Life **would** return to normal.*

Now freedom from her blackout watch reminds her day by day
that ration books, vic'try gardens, war bonds, and tinfoil
are set aside in thought and use as Lilies claim old strides;
at last they smile again to learn Belk's selling real silk hose,
and real butter's home again.

1946

Narcissus: Queen of the T.E.A. Room

From *The Dispatch*, Friday, March 20, 1946

Sandy Hills Curiosity peaked this week at the news about refurbishing the second floor space of the old pharmacy and drug store building, constructed in 1919 and occupied in 1920, by owners Drs. Frank Thomas, Ted Emory, and Forrest Armstrong. The pharmacists co-owned the property until the three retired and went out of business in 1945, with Dr. Emory retaining ownership.

Sidney Rollins and son, well-regarded gardeners, after a search for the perfect climate for growing exquisite flowers, as well as more familiar blooms, have said that Sandy Hills is the answer. This father-son duo will use the leased ground-floor quarters as an arranging station for floral designs. In the same vicinity, they will also grow and manage indoor gardens.

From *The Dispatch*, Monday, March 23, 1946

Sandy Hills On Friday, March 20, a notice appeared in *The Dispatch*, reporting future possibilities for an attractive business area on the second floor of the old pharmacy building downtown. Reports indicate Realtors Albertson and Montgomery of Charlotte are buying the building, pending completion of arrangements between them and the seller, Dr. Ted Emory. An agreement reached last week leased the lower floor to the flower growers; however, *The Dispatch* has learned that the second story interests will opt for a two-year lease to be extended if necessary, according to Dr. Emory.

Sandy Hillites showed few regrets at the final closing of the building, possibly because of its architecture. But the mystery is that nobody seemed to know why the second floor was among the town's major topics of conversation. Did the space accommodate a secretive band of brothers or a meeting place for the ladies? Some reported having seen a kitchen there in the midst of surrounding rooms, suggesting that the area might have once housed tenants. *The Dispatch* has reported it was leaving no stone unturned in determining its history and what its future holds—if anything.

"Nar'ciss! Can you come here a minute and look at what's in the paper for heaven's sake?" Cora Lee was adamant.

"Honey, I got no time to read no paper. Can you just tell me what it says? I would kindly 'preciate that. I would. And don't call me Nar'ciss no more. I'm your mama and not your sister; don't you forget it."

"Sorry, Mama."

"O.K. now. What do it say?"

"Like I said, if you'll come to the kitchen table, I'll pour your coffee, butter your toast, and read you the paper. I'm tellin' ya: you need to see this."

"No more talk, Cora Lee; just read me the paper. No toast, just coffee," ordered Narcissus.

Cora Lee had not seen the earlier article about the florist and was reading the more pertinent news of her family's past. "Now, Mama, I remember you been in them second story rooms and know full well what they's all about. So tell somebody . . . ."

"And who would you want me to tell? Mayor McNeill? The preacher? The sheriff? How 'bout Marvin Steele?"

"Oh, Mama, you won't do. Think about it. I got to go next door and help O'Zella and Marvin with the wash. It's bein' Monday and all. See you at lunch . . . ."

"I'll have you a chicken sandwich on white bread."

"Reckon that chicken's still good? We cooked it yesterday, you know."

"Oh, Corey," said Narcissus as she almost ran to the telephone in the parlor. She stopped long enough to think again of whom to call about that second floor. She knew plenty, and she was going to spill it. In fact, no one was better acquainted with the old building than was Narcissus. If she were not already 77, going on 78, "they'd be plenty of people remembering me in that same kitchen up them stairs in that old barn."

Who in the world will I tell?" she said to the idle receiver. The telephone returned her call at that very moment, so she wasted no time claiming her right to the talkin' machine, as she called it. "Helloo," she said eagerly in a welcoming voice. How people loved this old dear who aged with the years but stayed so young in her demeanor.

Is this my friend Narcissus?" asked the voice. "I hope I can talk with you about something."

"Of course I remember you, friend. Just tell me your name and we'll talk." (Laughter over the wires on both ends.)

"I'm Patty Herring—your old buddy out at the college."

"Oh-h-h, it's Miss Patty. Honey, I miss you so bad! I'd rather talk to you than anybody I know. Come to see me next Sare'dy. You still know where I live? McNeill Street? We'll talk. So much to tell. To ask. Can't wait!"

"Of course I remember where you live," Patty chided. "In the meantime, take care, Narcissus. See you Saturday morning. Bye." So Patty Herring signed off, no hint of conversations to come.

At the end of the spring semester, Dr. Patty Herring had announced that she was dropping out of school. The *grande dame* of literature at the woman's college, so respected for its liberal arts emphasis, was dropping out of school? What?

"You're foolin' me!" Narcissus was incredulous. "There's got to be a reason, Miss Patty. Can you tell me?"

Patty laughed. "Well, remember I said 'at the end of the spring semester.' That simply means I'm taking a vacation from teaching summer school this year. That's all."

"But you always teach summer school. Somebody played a joke on you? Yo' tenure didn't go through!" 'Ciss was sure she had figured it all out.

The teachers know how rich life is: they'd rather teach than sing
or dance or sew or even paint a masterpiece or two,
but now and then one's heard to say, "If I could only type . . . ."
An office job, they think, lends oomph to them on downtown Main
keeping them at work all year.

They "toil" in chalky classrooms to teach six-year-olds to read, may
live in nearby "teacherage"—with peers—for meager rent. Their
students learn to multiply and race for best in class.
After 'rithmetic and reading, Miss Lily says, "Let's write,
but we don't know our cursive yet.

The two friends sat down on the couch in the parlor. "Narcssus," began Patty . . . . "I want to tell you some news: three of my teacher friends and I are planning for the summer, and—my goodness—there you are right in the midst of what we want to do. Will you think about joining us?"

"Who the other three, Miss Patty? And what are your plans? But first: you like your coffee black? Still? Will you try one of my lemon tarts?"

"Yes on both counts, Hon. So glad you haven't changed. But hurry back, please. Can't wait to hear what you think." After Patty sped 'Ciss on her way, she slipped off her shoes and relaxed, hopeful that Narcissus would want to add another year or two of work to her life.

The refreshments introduced a thoughtful time of including Narcissus in the teachers' plots and how they would involve her. She was surprised when Annabelle Teague rang the doobell almost an hour later. Narcissus glanced at her watch. It was 10:45.

"Well, this is a nice surprise. You're Miss Teague from the newspaper, aren't you? I'm Narcissus Lambeth. Come in, come in! So glad to meet you," assured the hostess. "And this is my good friend from the College, Dr. Patty Herring. She's a member of the English faculty.

Patty stood; the two visitors shook hands and spoke words previously exchanged by the two.

The press representative took the next opening: May I call you Narcissus, Mrs. Lambeth?"

Of course. It's the name I love to hear!" assured the hostess.

"It's a lovely name. And please call me Annabelle. I have jotted down some notes that should familiarize us with the status of things. Editor Linderman and I met last night in the good company of Patty and her three colleagues who were, even then, up to their ears with tea room plans for the second floor. And, by the way, the three teachers asked that their names not be revealed until they could notify their school supervisors. Dr. Emory was also present. Of course, he's the one negotiating for the sale of the building, although the other two doctors on the original "team" are being fully informed of the progress.

Patty decided Annabelle should know about 'Ciss's work at the College before retirement . . . .

Annabelle jumped in with "And, who, Narcissus, was in charge of event scheduling and planning big moments, such as graduation? Junior-Senior? Parents' Weekend?"

"Well, I did right smart of all that," admitted Nar'Ciss. Annabelle insisted, "Look at me, Narcissus. Who was basically in charge?"

"Well, me, I guess. Yes, it was me. That's how come I got my job in the first place: they hired me over there to be food planner and pastry chef. (They called it that. Not me.) I sort of arranged parties, too. The college hosted more parties. What times we had."

"So there! You've confirmed all I ever heard about you dear," said Patty. "Can you do it again?"

The questioner didn't get an answer for a few minutes. Finally:

"You all know how old I am?"

"Yes. Yes, we do. Does it matter?" asked Annabelle.

"No, ma'am. It don't matter a whit," declared the sought-after food planner and pastry chef. "'Scuse' me while I run fix us a cup o' potato soup and a salad . . . . And my daughter Corey has an old car. She'd get me there and pick me up. Do you really mean you want me? For this?"

"WHAT DO YOU THINK, NARCISSUS?" questioned the pair in the parlor.

From *The Dispatch* Monday, March 30, 1946
Good News for Sandy Hill's New Tea Room, Page 1
By Ben Linderman and Annabelle Teague Sandy Hills All the stones were turned during the weekend, and the mystery apparently was cleared of questions regarding the second story's tale of the long-orphaned old pharmacy building. The Dispatch learned Saturday night of significant progress in the final stages of the sale and the refurbishing to come. Then, on Sunday afternoon at 2:00 p.m. in the Sandy Hills High School Auditorium, concerned citizens and members of the local and area media represented the public in impressive numbers.

Attendees included Mayor McNeill, Dr. Patty Herring and her three teacher cohorts, who originated the idea for a small tea room and will likely serve as supervisory staff for the business, and Mrs. Narcissus Lambeth, experienced chef for a well-known former restaurant, and now being addressed as "The Lady of the Hour" for all the good ideas of her past successes.

Also present were the three pharmacists who occupied the building in question until their retirement a year ago. A surprise awaited Drs. Frank Thomas, Ted Emory, and Forrest Armstrong when Mrs. Lambeth made a motion to call the enterprise a T.E.A. room in honor of the three doctors whose last names began with the letters spelling out the new name. The vote was unanimous.

Dr. Emory originally bought the building from his colleagues and, as such, became the decision maker in the process. He has agreed to sell, refurbish the area, and support the tea room financially, as far as he and his accountant determine is possible.

A standing ovation showed appreciation to Dr. Emory, the women who originated the idea of a new tea room, and the town of Sandy Hills for its future support.

Annabelle Teague was still searching for a report on what in the world had so entertained Sandy Hills with dubious dealings in the pharmacy's unused space for a period too long past. "In a nutshell, the second floor—about 15 years ago—was what, Narcissus?" asked Annabelle.

Narcissus didn't hesitate. "May I tell you a true story? Some of it's about hard times."

Annabelle urged her on. "That's what we want, dear: the truth. What were the hard times like?

"Oh, you know what I mean, Miss Annabelle. The worst of 'em were at the beginning, the middle, and the never-ending end: that awful Depression. The Great one, you know—with a capital 'G'." Narcissus paused to dry her eyes with her handkerchief. "Then come—came—the second war, and we aren't yet recovered I don't believe. But that's just part of it.

"And?" Annabelle seemed impatient.

"Well, that whole upstairs was turned into a mean-spirited period for everybody. But let me go to the beginning. My husband Jesse was old and crippled. I took him there, and I don't know if he gambled or not. He certainly never come—came—home with money. And he never said if he lost any. But he did come home angry. Twice a week.

"I waited down in the drug store while he wuz with his buddies, but sometimes I went to the stairway and heard men shoutin' at each other, callin' their friends awful names, drinkin' beer 'n' all, fightin'. I do think sometimes they fought. Hard. I usually cried myself to sleep ev'ry one of them nights. Jesse died durin' the night after a gamblin' binge. But he was poorly anyway." They waited a minute for Narcussus to regain her composure.

"Do you have other criticism, Hon?" Patty was also upset. "Well, some, I guess. Somebody hosted a teenagers' dance up there every Saturday night. I was not there. They was loud, so

I heard, but I didn't hear of no fightin', just loud with the music and some underage drinkin'. That might be a little iffy."

From The Dispatch, Wednesday, April 9, 1946
Sandy Hills At the monthly meeting of the Town Council last night, answers regarding the over-discussed second floor of the former pharmacy building were unveiled, and, according to Mayor Roark, a very short statement is sufficient; the mayor reported, "We have just learned from an eye-witness account that perceived problems occurred in the pharmacy building, a decade ago, on Tuesday, Thursday, and Saturday nights. While the pharmacy below would have been open, the upper portion of the building was supervised by rotating night watchmen who "overlooked" the Council's directives to "disallow gambling and alcohol in unsupervised public places." Inasmuch as the problems occurred ten or more years prior to current concerns, the Council voted not to press charges. The "Statute of Limitations" was the phrase suggested by Ralph Bowman, City Engineer. A unanimous vote followed.

The first six days in the T.E.A. Room were phenomenal. Crowds, good food, worthy tips, laughter, banana pudding . . . . The list continued. After the restaurant cleared of customers on Friday afternoon, Narcissus approached Patty Herring:
"Miss Patty, can you spare a minute?"
"Of course, 'Ciss. What's on your mind?"
"Only that we need a young waitress. I believe it would help to have some younger legs waiting tables—taking orders, serving food, smiling sweetly . . . ."
Patty, quick to reply, agreed heartily. "You always hit the nail on the head. I can tell that you have such a person in mind already. Right?"
"You read me like a book. Yes! Yes I do. There's a young girl—about 16—who lives next door to me. Her name is Glory Steele, and she's a smart, trustworthy young lady. Pretty, mannerly. Now here's the thing, professor . . . ."
"Hold it, Narcissus. What are you about to say next?" Patty liked to tease her old friend.

"Well, here's the thing: She's a couple of years too early for college, but, more than life, she wants to be a writer. Is there anything we could do to encourage her?"

"Can you bring her in for an interview Monday? I'd personally like to tutor her and understand just how eager she is to excel. At her age, though, she must obtain a worker's permit before we can actually employ her as a waitress. I'll find out where she needs to apply and take her there. We could give her lunch and stay a little while to get to know her." Patty looked pleased that teaching had not entirely left her for the summer.

"Thank you, thank you!" exclaimed Narcissus. "It'll work. I know it will."

Because the tea room was not open on Sundays, Narcissus was glad to have the day to talk with Glory. The young lady was delighted at the prospects that might help her learn outside as well as in class. As a matter of fact, she told Narcissus that she would take Miss Patty the first poem she ever wrote as a start. "Good girl," said her current "mentor" (Glory's proudest word).

The young girl was troubled in a way that she didn't want to ask her neighbor, so she saved the big question to discuss with Dr. Herring, her tutor-to-be: "Ma'am, I jus' want to know for sure that I could wait on white folks. Don't none of my folks eat here, do they?"

"Oh, my dear, what a sad thing you've asked me, and I don't know what to tell you but that your fine neighbor, Narcissus, works here, and she's certainly no problem." Patty was shaken by the question.

Glory continued, "But, ma'am, she cooks, don't she? There's a big difference in cookin' and conversin' with the customers."

"I don't think there will be a problem, Glory, so let's just give it a day and see how it goes. I wouldn't have you hurt for anything in the world. But if it happened, it would hurt . . . ."

"Oh, yes'm. It would. But it's gotta happen some time. Listen. This talkin' reminds me of my poem. Can I read it now?"

"Please do, Honey. I can't wait."

Glory fumbled in a notebook and found her copy. She was smart to have been so organized, thought Patty.

"Here goes, ma'am. I shoulda made you a copy, but I'll give you this one, if you like it. Here goes":

GOD'S LITTLE BLACK LAMB

My skin is black, but that's who I am.
Strange: Inside, I can't see my color.
When Mom says I'm God's Little Black Lamb,
Does that mean I'm brighter? Or duller?
I'll write books like the Bronte Sisters,
Or reach the whole world with my love song.
And black or white, Misses or Misters
Arm in arm, we're sure to get along.
By Glory Steele, 1942

"Glory! You wrote that? How old were you in 1942? Only eleven? Come here, child, and let me give you a hug!" Patty was ecstatic. Glory, beaming, returned the hug and proudly handed the printed copy of "God's Little Black Lamb" to her tutor.

"Now, let's keep the poem before us, and I want you to tell me what's good about it? What did I get excited about?" asked Pattie.

"All I know is you seemed to like it, Ma'am," said Glory. "An' I'm real glad about that."

"But let's look at each line. You set out to make it rhyme, did you?"

"Oh, yes'm."

"Why?"

"Well, back then, I thought it had to rhyme to be a poem," Glory had good answers.

"And when did you discover that there's more to a poem than its rhyme?" Miss Patty asked a good question.

"Well," started the young poet . . . . "uh, there's one thing I don't really understand."

"Have you included it in 'God's Little Lamb' Glory?"

"Yes'm, but I didn't know it until Miss Owens told me."

"Wait! You're not talking about Janet Owens, are you?"

Well, I am really. She's my tenth grade English teacher. You know her?"

"**Do** I? She's an old friend from other days and places of teaching. Does she live in Sandy Hills?" Patty was as pleased as she was surprised.

"I think so, but I don't know where at."

"That's fine, dear. I'll look up my old friend." Patty decided not to mention the "at" preposition. "We're running out of time, Glory. All right with you if we talk about 'meter' tomorrow?"

Glory grinned. "It's time for Miss Cora Lee to pick her mama and me up anyway," she said, as she gathered her belongings. After a pause, she said, "Miss Patty, I didn't want to tell you 'no.'"

"No to what, dear? Is something wrong?"

"Well, maybe. I don't really know. My mama told me to forget the worker's permit we was talking about. She didn't want me serving white folks—not 'cause we don't like 'em, but she's afraid they won't like for us to serve them, you know."

"Glory, bless you. I'm so sorry you and your mom have this concern. You're too fine, too precious, to face the hurt. Let the literary world get to know you, dear. I'm so thankful I do. But we all need to be watching and listening for you."

By mid-June Sandy Hills underwent the worst heat wave in the memory of anyone who would talk about it. The T.E.A. Room stalwarts were exhausted by the time breakfast was over, even if the early morning crowd had dwindled noticeably. On Mondays and Tuesdays, the men of early morning outnumbered the women, because, as some suggested, the men had pretty much washed their hands of Monday wash day; and, for that matter, Tuesdays, too, were in a slump. "No fire in their iron," one was heard to say.

Poor Narcissus was suffering from heat "like I ain't never felt." Through it all, the three sponsoring teachers carried through by taking turns with preparing as well as cleaning.

Finally, Narcissus was "simply unable to come in that heat and walk up them stairs" before having to cook. She was out three weeks "from heat exhaustion," said her doctor. Cora Lee made the decision: "Mama has to retire." And Mama didn't resist at all. It was not easy to employ another cook of the one just retired.

The heat was only one of the difficulties. The teachers, Patty, Virginia, and Toni had no claim to fame in that regard. It soon became clear that one reason the so anticipated tea room was at odds with popularity was that several new eating places had been added to Sandy Hills with the coming of Camp Snyderman. "Let's face it," said Patty.

The attractive rooms remodeled for women's meetings, such as book clubs, were empty usually. When Virginia called officers of the seven such clubs in town, six of them claimed, "We've become accustomed to meeting in homes, but thank you." The seventh one was the oldest one on record, and "Our women just can't walk up those high steps to the second floor. I'm sorry."

"Don't anybody even mention an elevator," Patty warned. All laughed at the idea.

The final decision came in August when Dr. Emory visited one Friday to "apologize from the depth of my heart, but I can't complete my offer to finance the T.E.A. room any longer. My buyers have had to declare bankruptcy . . . ."

"Say no more," offered Patty Herring, originator of the idea. Is it all right with you, Dr. Emory, if we declare loss of lease?"

Relief washed over the financier's face. "Yes, Dr. Herring, yes. Will you, the founders, meet with my attorney and me here on Monday?"

News spread so swiftly that The Dispatch announced the closing (nobody called it a failure) August 13, 1946, in a short paragraph on page 2.

1948

Dinner on the Grounds

The title sounds very much like a family reunion is about to take place somewhere or a church will be celebrating a notable anniversary or the White House is about to exonerate a captured turkey at Thanksgiving.

None of the above was the case. Margaret and Edward Spencer and their six children sent invitations to Mags' and Ed's 30th wedding anniversary celebration on the next Sunday after church. It read, "Dinner on the Grounds at the Spencers' home."

On the big day, Ed and Mags cornered Lily and Lil to insist they ride with them to their country place about ten miles down the hill from the church house, even though other drivers could have escorted the two back to town and saved the Spencers a return trip; however, the celebrants were determined, and everybody gets his/her own way on the 30th anniversary of wedded bliss, *n'est-ce pas*?

Bob, Ben, and William, the 20-year-old Spencer triplets, drove themselves, being over 16 and all, in a recent birthday gift from their family—a used green Ford—while the girls stayed at home to set an outdoor table for lunch. LUNCH? OR FEAST?

Mags was a litle antsy about how her food plans would turn out, even though two of the girls were old enough and certainly qualified to get a worthy meal on the table—even on a wedding anniversary.

Lily sat back next to the barely open rear window, where the breeze from her happiest season teased her hair and triggered some memories of the few months that she was Ed Spencer's right hand. That job, she thought, was a pleasant one, which helped struggling farmers qualify for government loans in the ongoing scarcity of necessary funds.

In her thoughtful state, Lily was startled when the car suddenly lost power. Even Mags jumped awake in the front seat, and delivered a quick explanation: "Listen, folks, Ed can't let his old habit lapse a single time. Lily, I'm sure you remember when a hill of any significance would lead him to save gas. Just cut off the switch and coast down hill. Remember?"

"I do indeed," answered Lily, laughing at how she'd jump every time the little difference in sound and speed would occur. She recalled how Mr. Spencer not only enjoyed startling his passengers as the car headed silently down the steep grade, but his patriotism was the inspiration to save fuel, rationed as it had been for so long.

He was also quite funny. Lily recalled traveling with him one morning on business. They had already reached their destination in the low country of coastal South Carolina—a very small village near Charleston—where the "Two Coasts Seminar" would be held. Ed said, "You want to hear an interesting accent?" Before she could answer, he lowered the window on his side and called to a big man in overalls, who was concentrating on designing a basket of "sivvy be-ans" for art imminent curb market. "Hey, mister, could you tell me how to get to McClellanville?

The man removed his hat as if to ponder a moment. Finally, he answered, "Suh, you's ther right now. This very minute. Enjoy yo' stay."

"Thank you, sir," said Ed, as he drove away, perfectly solemn. Lily laughed aloud at Mr. Spencer's wit back in those days. He was so taken aback at the man's reply—thinking all along the stranger would be speaking Gullah—that he had no idea how to laugh at himself.

So ensconced in that reverie, Lily didn't even notice when he turned the car key again, stepped on the gas pedal, picked up speed, and estimated, as he always did, how much fuel he had just saved.

When the two story white house on the next hill appeared in the distance, Mags was obviously pleased. "There she is, Eddy, our honeymoon cottage. And, oh, my goodness, look at all the children!"

"Well, we did include some youngsters in our plans, didn't we?" mumbled Ed. "You're not telling me we want more, are you?"

"Oh, dear, don't be funny. Have you stopped counting the grandchildren we already have?"

They pulled into the lengthy driveway leading from highway to carport up by the front porch. The clapping of many hands and cheering of happy voices warmly greeted the celebrants—as did an unobtrusive "For Sale" sign—up close to the house. Mags' voice, sweet as it was, was too soft for the eldest daughter, Margaret, to hear and come running, but the word got as far as the table where the namesake was frantically arranging food and utensils. "Give me 30 minutes, Mama," she called. "We'll eat at one o'clock, I promise."

The triplets and their two younger sisters brought out chairs, drums, guitars, horns, and a keyboard, announcing, "Let the entertainment begin."

"Play us some church music, now boys 'n' girls," Daddy Ed called through his amplified sound system (hands cupped around his mouth). The musicians switched immediately from war songs to all five verses of "Just As I Am" before the crowd called for "Jesus Loves Me," and then wanted "something peppy" like "Bringing in the Sheaves."

After the plentiful meal, consisting of every edible meat, starch, vegetable, salad, dessert, and soft drink available to the public, Edward Spencer, the groom, called for the microphone. He wasn't usually a speech maker, but that day, he was eloquent:

> Dear Family and Friends, my family is the essence of our celebration, and you, friends, have held us up in the *agape* love of our Lord. Mags and I have been married all of 30 years today, and we remember repledging our joined lives to God just four years later as our first child was born.

I love my Mags more today than I did then, although that's a lot to say. She has given me six beautiful children and all the love that an old Sandy Hills boy could hope for. I love you, Margaret McNeil Spencer, and always will. I have an anniversary gift for you, even though you pretty much paid for it your sweet self. *(Laughter).* That's good, good friends, glad to hear you laughing.

This will be a surprise to most of you—even our youngsters, except that our first-born, Edward Raymond, Spemcer, Jr., and Nancy, his lovely bride of five years, have made a gesture that we will delight in. And, Mags, I'm sorry not to have discussed this with you (more laughter), but I know you well enough to say, without reservation, you'll be jumping for joy.

"Ray, you and Nancy take the mike, PLEASE."

The oldest of the Spencer offspring and his wife came to the microphone. Ray spoke:

Thanks, Pops. Happy anniversary! Um, you, too, Mom. What we offer is a surprise to us as well as to you. I was born loving this house, and Nancy knows it well enough to love it, too. Since we were in college together, we've planned to talk to our folks about our buying it—for just us and whatever family we might produce—but not until we could make a fair deal with and for you. Here goes: Last week, we and dad talked to our realtor, and we've made a down payment with an option to buy it when you make the arrangements that you've hoped would come true for half a century, huh Mom?

Ed Spencer returned to the microphone, took it from his wife, who was about to speak. (But not this time.)

When I mentioned that Mags had almost paid for this house herself, let me explain briefly. I need not mention the sad economic pain we've all suffered recently. I also don't have to remind you what Mags has been doing for years even before I came into her life.

    She has sold cleaning products, her car serving as her office for an unbelievable number of years. She has saved every dollar of her Saturday practice of delivering orders by automobile. It was our plan from the beginning. Mags thanks God for making the impossible possible. I praise Him for every minute of every day with her and our children. You've heard the story—about 90 percent of you have, anyway—and I will confirm your thoughts: Tomorrow, Lord willing, I—Mags, too—will meet the realtor representing the old Markham home, located a block from our church, and make our down payment for it, plus almost the total amount we need to buy it outright. We've wanted that house for years. Now is the time. It's all yours, Mags. *(applause, applause)*

Mags beamed as she claimed the microphone for her "unprepared" remarks:

    Thank you, dear. If I had not married a wise man, this could not be. I'm not greatly surprised that Ray and Nancy will buy this honeymoon house that I, too, love and cherish. But, through the years, I've been shown by the Lord children will see what we've seen about the importance of their "young'uns" (excuse my French!) growing up where they'll gain most from their environment—*school, neighborhood, close community, and not the least of which is their church.* Not that ours kids have suffered. They have all done well. Edward has seen to that, but I believe the Lord has wanted us to be closer to the church we love, and the Markham house is only half a block from it. Thank you, Lord, for the money . . . And for letting me speak for a second or two.

Bob, Ben, and William, the triplets, made a motion to strike up the band. Ben said over the microphone, "Dry your tears. Mama's speech was wonderful, but not for crying. Let's stand now and sing 'Bringing in the Sheaves,' and do what we've all done lately—Rejoice."

The guests stood, singing lustily, filling in words they didn't know of the old hymn, while the younger folk played a rousing game of croquet in the back yard.

WWII flight nurse collected wounded from Okinawa

Dawn M. Kurry

Margaret Lucille Covington was born in 1919. Her friends know her as Lou. She is a World War II veteran and will be attending the Flight of Honor to Washington, D.C., with other WWII veterans. Her close friend Myra Dean will accompany her as her guardian.

Many soldiers made it back from foreign battlefields due to flight nurses in the Navy Nurse Corps.

Covington was one of the first to join the Navy as a nurse. She was stationed in Guam, where her plane, a Douglas Aircraft hospital plane, would fly into Okinawa. The flight nurse, along with a few corpsmen, had 45 minutes to drop off supplies and cargo and to load up injured soldiers.

"We were just busy," she said. "There were injuries everywhere. We took the most injured, and triaged them. We took enemy fire. There was fighting all around us."

Covington landed on the beaches of Okinawa the day of the invasion.

"I remember how wonderful the patients were," she said. "They were so grateful."

The soldiers were placed on stretchers and stacked in the plane. Covington said they didn't complain and were friendly and thankful for the help. She said penicillin has just come out, and to administer it, she would often have to climb up the stacked stretchers and hang on with one hand while injecting with another.

Covington said when she signed up she had never flown on a plane before, and it made her throw up. The plane had to be flown from a certain altitude because the cabin wasn't yet pressurized.

"We had head injuries which you had to be careful with, and we had broken bones and shrapnel wounds. We flew them to Guam. It took about eight hours. I never had a complaint. We lost one or two but we took them just in case. A lot we left there (on the battlefield), because it was better. You knew it was the best thing, because they wouldn't make the trip."

Covington is a Rockingham native, and graduated high school here. She pursued her nursing career, and the path led her to the Navy. The Navy sent her back to school after her one-year station in Guam, to the University of Colorado, where she earned her bachelor's degree in nursing. She went from Guam to California, where she received patients off of ships coming home from the South Pacific. She also served as a hospital supervisor. She was instrumental in the building and establishment of a Naval hospital in Puerto Rico, and, on a clear day could see Cuba from where she was stationed. She was home during the Cuban Missile Crisis, and rushed back to Puerto Rico because she felt she may be needed to receive the wounded.

Covington served as a Navy recruiter during the '50s and early '60s in Raleigh but didn't enjoy it.

"I didn't like paperwork," she said. "I didn't want to sit behind a desk." She was discharged at Portsmouth, but only after achieving the rank of Commander, which was rare for women at that time.

"I was up for Captain but I wanted to come home," she said. I didn't want to give it another three or four years."

Although no longer in the Navy, her career as a nurse didn't end. Covington went on to teach nursing at RCC and SCC and served as chair of the department.

She has been active in her retirement as well. According to Dean, Covington delivered Meals on Wheels well into her 80s. She has been actively involved with her church and community. She now resides in Scotia Village in Laurinburg, and has given lectures for veterans on Veterans Day and other veteran functions.

"It's really nice for Rotary to do this for the veterans," said Dean.

The Flight of Honor to Washington, D.C., leaves on Sept. 17. The WWII veterans will visit the WWII memorials and sight-see in Washington, D.C., while being pampered by guardians who have volunteered their time to ensure the veterans are cared for and well hydrated. The trip is sponsored by Rotary International, local veterans and veterans organizations and donations from the public. The trip is no cost to the veterans that attend.

Note: This story of Margaret Lucille Covington, flight nurse in the Pacific Theater during World War II, is true, as reported in the *Richmond County Daily Journal* of September 9, 2011. It is reprinted with the kind permission of *Journal* Editor John Charles Robbins, staff writer Dawn M. Kurry, and of Commander Covington, as well.

It is the one true account in this collection of final stories about the "human lilies" who "toiled" and "spun" during some of the most difficult periods in our culture; i.e., World Wars I and II and the Great Depression, each of which historical era changed life as it was lived then.

The Last Word

From Another Lily

And now another prominent lily of the same species but a generation later spins and toils among other lilies of the field. You will recognize this lily of today's field standing as one of the tallest and strongest and most peaceful of flowers in her garden or in the land of promise. She is clothed and labeled as a flower of purpose, deeply rooted in divinity and with an upward turned sunny bloom she reflects God's glory as pictured in the real process that one goes through on a walk to fulfillment. Her many rhizomes spreading from her roots provide hope for generations of lilies to come.

The true lily that she is has grown long narrow arms along the length of her stem arching out to gather nourishment and food which she so gladly shares with other lilies still in rhizome. She has been seen wearing many large flamboyant hats and bonnets along her journey. And she gladly accepts the colors, species and varieties of dress on all the other lilies that come into her field. Other lilies witness her strong stand by observing her many faithful perennial returns. Few lilies have seen her tears but more often it is she who is seen wiping the tears of other younger sprouted lilies reaching up for solace and comfort, as they gather near her feet, emerging in aerial growth from rhizomes or, as young buds formed by the sheathing leaves process of her strong stem.

Lily's own laden roots and she struggled to survive, her faith provided her with a plentiful fall of leaves to cover and meet her needs. With her head to the sky she appears like a servant with her horizontally outspread green foliage providing needed shade and cool roots for other tender young lilies attempting to emerge from her rhizomes. Although she bends low to the ground in the breeze, her stems having been well staked and secured by generations of lilies before, protect her from high winds, giving her strength during storms as she combines her agility and tolerance and toils and spins with ease and grace. Not only is she observed spinning and toiling but dancing and singing. She has a melodious laughter set to music and shares it often with downtrodden lilies in her midst. At other times when she bows her head you might find her tendrils pointed vertical, upward spread toward the heavens, as she offers up her daily prayers to soar on a breeze toward Heaven. If you pass by this lily slowly or listen carefully as you stand near her, you may even hear a sweet soft whisper from her reminding us that there is real suffering in the life of the lily, necessary as an integral part of bringing us into rhythm and unity with God. These sensations are honest and true.

Her many perennial friends and family lilies might say that this genus lilum belongs to the family known as liliaceae, but not this lily . . . . she is an act of grace within herself.

Patricia Brewer

Lightning Source UK Ltd.
Milton Keynes UK
UKOW02f1026211015

261075UK00001B/94/P